COMBATING SEXUAL HARASSMENT IN THE WORKPLACE

Rohan Collier

Open University Press
Buckingham · Philadelphia

Open University Press
Celtic Court
22 Ballmoor
Buckingham
MK18 1XW

and
1900 Frost Road, Suite 101
Bristol, PA 19007, USA

First Published 1995

A catalogue record of this book is available from the British Library

ISBN   0 335 19082 0 (pb)   0 335 19083 9 (hb)

Library of Congress Cataloging-in-Publication Data
Collier, Rohan, 1945–
    Combating sexual harassment in the workplace / Rohan Collier.
        p.   cm.
    Includes bibliographical references and index.
    ISBN 0–335–19083–9 (hardback)   ISBN 0–335–19082–0 (paperback)
        1. Sexual harassment – Great Britain.   2. Sex discrimination in
    employment – Great Britain.   3. Sexual harassment – Law and
    legislation – European Union countries.   4. Sex discrimination in
    employment – Law and legislation – European Union countries.
    I. Title.
    HD6060.5.G7C647   1995
    331.13'3'0941–dc20   94–26386
                                                                    CIP

Typeset by Type Study, Scarborough
Printed in Great Britain by St Edmundsbury Press Ltd
Bury St Edmunds, Suffolk

COMBATING
SEXUAL HARASSMENT
IN THE WORKPLACE

MANAGING WORK AND ORGANIZATIONS SERIES

Edited by Graeme Salaman, Reader in Sociology in the Faculty of Social Sciences and the Open Business School, the Open University

Current and forthcoming titles include:

ACKNOWLEDGEMENTS

I am indebted to Suzanne Hickmott for early discussions on the content of the book. I am also indebted to Kathy Meade and Joe Collier for patiently reading and commenting on successions of drafts – much of the clarity in the book I owe to them. My thanks to Pam Ahluwalia for commenting on Chapter 3. Thanks also to City Centre which supported and encouraged my work on sexual harassment over four and a half years. I owe a special debt of thanks to the many women who shared with me their experiences of sexual harassment. It was through their bravery that I gained much of the insight that allowed me to write this book. Finally I would like to thank Wesleyan College, Macon (Georgia, USA) for giving me unlimited access to computer facilities during the final stages of the book's preparation.

Copyright permission has been obtained for using the equal opportunities policy and two sample harassment policies in the appendices. Permission has been obtained from City Centre for use of material in Chapter 2.

INTRODUCING AND DEFINING SEXUAL HARASSMENT

There can be few women in the UK who escape sexual harassment. Wolf whistles, page three girls, bottom pinching, glaring, forced intimacy and the fear of worse are all part of a woman's life and shape her place in our society. Indeed all this is so common that it has been seen as normal behaviour and so its pernicious effect on women essentially ignored. Women learn to expect sexual jibes and jokes and unwanted physical advances as part of life. But why should they? Why should they have to be continually on their guard in the street, at school or university, or at work? Why should they have to tolerate an unfair and undermining environment?

This book concentrates on just one aspect of sexual harassment – harassment in the workplace. It aims to offer practical advice on how employers and employees, institutions and unions can work together to bring about an environment free of sexual harassment. But to do this there must be a clear understanding of exactly what sexual harassment is, its effects, its legal setting and its roots and causes. Once these are known, one can consider the remedies. The book examines all these issues but first, in this chapter, I will consider the definition of sexual harassment, its incidence and its implications.

Sexual harassment in itself is not new, women have been

harassed at work ever since they have worked alongside men. In 1840 women working in the mines were described in a Royal Commission investigation as being constantly pressed for sexual favours by the men (Hurst 1986: 1). The term 'sexual harassment' however is relatively recent. It appeared in the United States of America during the 1970s following the women's movement. By the 1980s the term 'sexual harassment' had become commonly used in the UK. As more women have entered the workforce levels of sexual harassment appear to have increased either because more opportunities have arisen or because men have felt increasingly threatened and use sexual harassment to keep women in their place. In the 1950s the majority of women in Britain were not in paid employment. During the 1980s women's employment rose sharply. By 1992, approximately 70 per cent of women of working age were in paid employment, representing approximately half the workforce (EOC 1993). By 1995 more women will probably be in paid work than men. This rise in the number of women in employment has been paralleled by a rise in the number of complaints to the Equal Opportunities Commission about sex discrimination. In 1992 the number of complaints rose by 62 per cent over the previous year; most of this increase was due to complaints concerning maternity and pregnancy, but many also concerned sexual harassment. These figures are an indication of the barriers women face at work. Sexual harassment is just one of them.

Women have always found their own means for coping with sexual harassment either by laughing it off, ignoring it, or telling the harasser to 'shove off'. Only now is the responsibility for dealing with sexual harassment shifting from the individual to the organization. In the 1980s employers in the public sector started adopting sexual harassment policies, first local authorities, then other public service employers. Towards the end of the decade harassment policies were beginning to be adopted by the private sector.

What is sexual harassment?

Some definitions of sexual harassment simply list the types of behaviour which could constitute harassment. This is not as helpful as it may seem at first since the same piece of behaviour may be seen as harassment by one woman and not by another. Harassment has to be defined by the effect the behaviour has on the recipient:

> in practice, harassment is by its very nature 'experiential'. This means that the same behaviour may be interpreted in different ways by different people. Moreover some individuals may interpret identical behaviour practised by different people in very different ways.
>
> (Local Government Management Board 1993: 10)

Harassment is only harassment if it is felt to be so by the recipient woman. Such a definition is compatible with the legal assessment of harassment which depends on the effect of the behaviour on the woman's working conditions (see Chapter 3 on sexual harassment disadvantaging women). The most widely used definition of sexual harassment is that given by Michael Rubenstein: 'unwanted conduct of a sexual nature or conduct based on sex which is offensive to the recipient' (1992b: 2). The European Commission's Code of Practice (see Chapter 4) adopts the same definition adding that 'it is for each individual to determine what behaviour is acceptable to them and what they regard as offensive . . . It is the unwanted nature of the conduct which distinguishes sexual harassment from friendly behaviour, which is welcome and mutual' (1991). The code reminds readers that sexual harassment is quite different from romantic relationships that are consensual. Sexual harassment is neither 'romantic' nor 'sexy' as it is imposed on the recipient (European Commission 1993: 24). There are, however, gender differences here. Behaviours that would be seen by most women as offensive are often not seen as such by men. This would apply for example to touching (more women see this as 'sexual harassment') or jokes about sex. On the whole women describe a wider range of behaviours as potential harassment than men do (Gutek 1985). Men are also twice as likely to attribute sexual harassment to sexual desire than women are. Women are more likely to attribute it to power play. Carrie Herbert (1992) draws a distinction between sexual harassment and sexual hassle, the latter being the result of, for example, the crush a student has for a

3

teacher. She argues that the difference lies in the fact that the crush 'cannot destroy self-esteem or endanger intellectual self-confidence. There is no threat for the professor of retaliation in the form of withheld recommendations, punitive treatment or fear of getting unfair low grades. Ultimately the professor has the power to control the situation' (1992: 24). The reverse situation is of course quite different, a tutor does wield immense power over a student and similar behaviour by a tutor towards a student would count as harassment. This also fits the legal definition mentioned above, for example, that harassment is measured by the impact of the behaviour on the recipient particularly in terms of her conditions of work. Herbert also distinguishes sexual harassment from bullying by saying that bullying, which is also based on power differences and is also threatening and humiliating, is nevertheless different because it 'is in no way connected with sexual inequality' (1992: 23).

Although it is not possible to identify types of behaviour that could be termed unequivocally 'sexual harassment' it is possible to describe the sorts of behaviour which might be seen as harassment by some women. These include physical conduct such as touching, pinching, physical actions which intimidate or embarrass (leering, whistling, suggestive gestures), physical sexual advances and assault; verbal conduct such as statements which are felt as insults, jokes of a derogatory nature, threatening or obscene language, verbal sexual advances; offensive materials which are seen to degrade or offend such as pornographic pictures, badges or graffiti. One celebrated example of sexual harassment was revealed in the harassment case brought by Anita Hill against Judge Clarence Thomas in 1991 where Hill alleged that three months after she started work, Thomas invited her out. When she refused, he started pestering her with repeated invitations, telling her about pornographic movies he had seen and describing his fantasies: 'he discussed people with large penises or breasts, he told me graphically of his own sexual prowess' (quoted in *Observer* 1991: 23). Thomas also made comments such as 'who put pubic hair on my Coke?', referred to his penis as 'larger than usual' and claimed that he had given women pleasure with oral sex.

Another more recent example was given in the *British Medical*

Journal (1992). Here an anonymous doctor described the kind of behaviour junior women doctors have to put up with: an older doctor said to her one day 'you have lost a lot of weight. Especially here' and with both hands he clutched her buttocks and squeezed. She also refers to a registrar who was forever wolf whistling down corridors, 'flicking up skirts, bringing his sexual exploits into the conversation, brushing against nurses' bodies, and entering the female senior house officers' rooms at night offering to go to bed with them'. Other male doctors are described as 'having their eyes fixed at chest level'. The medical school rugby club 'publicly displayed videos of women performing oral sex on men at the freshers' fair' and 'teachers showed pornographic pin-ups in surgery and gynaecology lectures'. All these are clear examples of the type of behaviour many women would see as sexual harassment. Recently a new type of behaviour can be added to the list: computer pornography. This is distributed mainly through the computer bulletin boards, which with the right software and a modem enable people to leave messages for each other. An example quoted in the *Campaign Against Pornography Newsletter* (1992: 5) is of 'a man who put on screen a digitised photo of a woman performing fellatio and was invited to comment on the size of the man's "equipment"'. This type of harassment is becoming increasingly frequent at universities – the University of Central Lancashire, for instance, dealt with nine cases of computer pornography in one year (1991 to 1992). In Lancashire these were usually in text form but sometimes in graphics and were being used to displace women's work on the computer by substituting it for the pornographic message (Campaign Against Pornography 1992).

Incidence of sexual harassment

There have now been a number of surveys on the incidence, forms and effects of sexual harassment. Results can vary depending on the questions being asked. When women were asked in a NOP survey for the *Independent on Sunday* in October 1991, whether they had suffered sexual harassment the response was quite low (one in six replied 'yes') but when asked if they have experienced certain types of behaviour and found them offensive women's responses are much higher (on average a third will say 'yes'). This difference – from one in six to one in three – arises because not all people understand what sexual harassment means. If the NOP figures were taken as correct this would mean that approximately two million women in Britain have experienced sexual harassment. From other studies mentioned below this is an underestimate.

Sexual harassment occurs in virtually all workplaces to a varying degree. It is not possible to tell the extent of sexual harassment in an organization simply by looking at the number and nature of complaints. Complaints only represent those willing to report and many incidents go unreported (see below). This is particularly true if the organization has no harassment policy, in these instances the underreporting is likely to be worse. People will only complain if they know they will be supported in their complaint (e.g., if there is a fully implemented and publicized sexual harassment policy). The only way to find out how widespread sexual harassment is in any organization is to conduct an anonymous survey of everyone in the workforce. A sample survey can be found in Michael Rubenstein's *Preventing and Remedying Sexual Harassment at Work* (1992b).

How widespread is sexual harassment?

In spite of low reporting, surveys show that sexual harassment is widespread and a major problem in all organizations. A Manchester School of Management survey by Marilyn Davidson and Jill Earnshaw (1991) of personnel directors showed that few had sexual harassment cases brought to their attention. Indeed 65 per cent of respondents had no incidents reported to them at all in the past year. At the same time, 65 per cent of the personnel directors surveyed thought that between 70 and 100 per cent of sexual harassment incidents were never reported. This belief is probably correct if one looks at surveys of employees. I once gave a talk to a group of students. The college secretary was in the audience. His remark that there were no cases of sexual harassment at his institution was greeted by incredulous laughter by the women in the audience.

According to the Industrial Society survey (1993) just over half of working women experience sexual harassment. This level of harassment occurred across most organizations and at most levels (rarely however at executive/director level). This figure is similar to figures in most other surveys: in the Alfred Marks Survey (1991), 47 per cent of women and 14 per cent of men had experienced sexual harassment. London Buses Ltd did a survey in 1991 which showed that 50 per cent of women had substantial experience of harassment. In some parts of London 80 per cent of women said they had experienced harassment (compared with 28 per cent of men) and 40 per cent had been subjected to 'uninvited and deliberate touching of intimate parts of the body' (compared with 4 per cent of men). Women commented: 'My friends outside work thought it was one of those things I would have to expect working in a bus garage – just like On the Buses' or 'I thought everybody would blame me or tell me it was just part of the job' (London Buses Ltd 1991).

The Confederation of Health Service Employees (COHSE) in 1991 showed that out of a total of 140 people, 98 women and 16 men had been sexually harassed, 11 women and 15 men had not experienced harassment. The men who had experienced harassment did not find it the devastating experience women did.

A survey of students carried out by the Student's Union at Durham University in 1992 (*Times Higher Education Supplement* 1992) found that more than two-thirds of women students had experienced unwelcome sexual attention.

A study about sex discrimination in the police service was carried out by Her Majesty's Inspectorate of Constabulary in 1992 in 12 out of the 43 police forces (*Equal Opportunities in the Police Service*). The survey showed that women in the police force were suffering persistent sexual harassment of one kind or another (9 out of 10 women). There was also evidence that physical harassment brought to the attention of supervisors had not been dealt with (Her Majesty's Inspectorate of Constabulary 1993).

What form does sexual harassment take?

Derogatory remarks, suggestive looks and sexual comments are the most common forms of sexual harassment. The Industrial

Society survey (1993) showed that the most frequent form of harassment concerned naming, that is where women colleagues were referred to as 'girl', 'darling' or 'love' (70 per cent). The second most common form of harassment was comments about clothing and looks (60 per cent), the third was suggestive looks – looking a person up and down (60 per cent) – and then sexual innuendoes or stories (55 per cent), and touching (20 per cent).

The Alfred Marks survey (1991) found that the most common forms of harassment were touching or patting, regular sexual remarks or jokes, being eyed up and down and suggestive looks at parts of the body.

After the 1993 BBC series *Making Advances* (BBC 1993), the BBC ran a help line. In their evaluation of those who called they found that the most common form of harassment was verbal abuse (95 per cent of women who called the help line and 74 per cent of men who called); 41 per cent of women had experienced sexual assault (and 33 per cent of men) and 31 per cent of women had been subjected to obscene gestures (19 per cent of men); 5 per cent of women had been offended by the use of pornography at work (no men); 16 per cent of women and 14 per cent of men had been subjected to sexual blackmail; 8.5 per cent of women had been raped (no men).

In the COHSE survey (1991) 86 per cent of respondents stated that harassment took the form of unwanted suggestive looks or remarks, 67 per cent had been subjected to unwanted pressure for dates, 16 per cent to pressure for sexual favours. In addition some people had been locked in a room with the harasser, experienced physical assault and attempted rape.

The survey of students at Durham University (*Times Higher Education Supplement* 1992) found that 53 per cent experienced 'eyeing up'. The next most common experience was sexual remarks followed by brushing against the body, touching and grabbing. Rape was experienced by 3 per cent and attempted rape by 7 per cent.

In the police survey (Her Majesty's Inspectorate of Constabulary 1993) 6 per cent of women had experienced serious sexual assaults and 30 per cent had been pinched or touched. One in five were pestered for unwanted dates.

Who gets harassed?

It is largely women who get harassed. Those women who are in junior jobs or serving and caring jobs are more likely than other women to be harassed. Lesbians and gay men experience more harassment than heterosexuals.

In the Industrial Society survey (1993) fewer than 7 per cent of those harassed were men. The Alfred Marks survey (1991) showed that 62 per cent of the victims were women. In the COHSE survey (1991) student nurses seemed to face much more harassment than anyone else in the health service, and they all feared that if they reported incidents this could affect their assessment. Gay staff also reported harassment.

Of the women who called the BBC programme *Making Advances'* help line most were secretaries or administrative staff, the next most common groups (in descending order) were students, nurses or carers, sales assistants, managers, factory workers, teachers, receptionists and social workers. In addition to this a few worked in traditional 'male' occupations: computing, engineering, the police, prisons, British Rail and the army. Of the men who called many were managers or directors enquiring about information on good workplace practice. Of those who were calling about harassment 10 per cent were non-white (which is a higher percentage than in the population) and 10 per cent were gay men.

Lesbians and gay men often get harassed at work. A survey, *Less Equal than Others*, done by the gay lobbying group Stonewall in 1993 showed that one in two lesbians and gay men had been harassed at work, 48 per cent of these specifically because of their sexuality. Harassment of lesbians and gay men takes the form of jokes or teasing (79 per cent), homophobic abuse (51 per cent), aggressive questioning (41 per cent), threats (14 per cent) and physical violence (5 per cent).

Can men be sexually harassed? Although men as well as women get sexually harassed, it is overwhelmingly women who experience harassment (neither the Equal Opportunities Commission nor the unions, nor Women Against Sexual Harassment report many complaints from men). For women, sexual harassment can always ultimately mean rape, this cannot be the case for men being harassed by women; 'whilst women and girls may fear that sexual harassment could escalate and ultimately end in rape, men experiencing sexual hassle carry with them neither the dread, nor the potential and inherent intimidation of this ultimate violation' (Herbert 1992: 24). Carrie Herbert, along with other authors, argues that men cannot be sexually harassed:

> Sexual harassment is dependent on the combined effect of two forms of power: individual (or personal) power, and institutional power . . . Therefore any sexist behaviour perpetrated by a woman towards a man, whilst embarrassing, humiliating and unwanted, cannot and does not have the same degree of authority as sexual harassment.
>
> (Herbert, 1992: 12)

However, although their experience is different men are harassed on occasion at work (often by other men) and in law this can count as sexual harassment. I take the view that men can experience sexual harassment but this experience is qualitatively different and therefore has a different meaning from the harassment a woman would experience. A survey done by MORI for the GMB (General and Municipal Boilermaker's union) showed that although men and women have similar views on what constitutes harassment there are two major points of difference in their views: women experience sexual harassment in terms of power and men do not, the other difference is that women see being asked to make the tea and run errands as serious sexual harassment and men do not (quoted in *Equal Opportunities Review* 1992b). Unlike Michael Crichton's (author of *Jurassic Park*) novel *Disclosure*, where the hero is sexually harassed by his female boss, men are very rarely harassed by their bosses (unlike women) but experience harassment if they are working in a female-dominated environment. Even then their experience is different, according to the agony aunt Claire Rayner, their main worry is 'not being able to get it up' (quoted in The *Guardian*: 2, 21 January 1994, pp. 2–3.). Throughout this book I shall therefore, unless indicated otherwise, assume the harasser is male and the person harassed female.

Who are the harassers?

Harassers are, on the whole, men either of similar or higher status to the person being harassed. Physical harassment is more likely to come from superiors than from colleagues or juniors. The Industrial Society survey (1993) revealed that most harassers, for all forms of harassment, were either peers (60 to 70 per cent) or managers (around 30 per cent). Harassment by subordinates was similar to that of peers and managers except in the area of touching: 'This suggests that those with some sense of control or power over harassees are more likely to take direct advantage of it by harassing in a more intimate way' (1993: xviii).

The Alfred Marks Bureau (1991) found that 59 per cent of the harassers were senior staff other than immediate bosses, 55 per cent were colleagues and 43 per cent were immediate bosses.

At the BBC help line in 1993, 93 per cent of harassers of women were male and 7 per cent female, 65 per cent were sexually harassed by their boss and 35 per cent by colleagues. Of male callers, 58 per cent had been harassed by women and 42 per cent by men. Where men were harassed by women it was often in workplaces where men were in a minority. Many of the men who were harassed were also subjected to racial or homophobic abuse. Men were harassed equally by their colleagues and their bosses.

In the COHSE Survey (1991), complaints were mainly against senior staff and doctors. Some of the comments made during the survey were: 'It was inferred that one should expect abuse from doctors'. 'We have a consultant who is generally free with his hands . . . if he were a porter he would have been sacked – but as a consultant he gets away with it'. Many complaints were also against members of the public.

At Durham University (*Times Higher Education Supplement* 1992) most of the perpetrators were students (51 per cent), 42 per cent were people outside the university, 7 per cent were academic staff and 3 per cent were college staff.

What are the effects of sexual harassment?

All surveys show that sexual harassment has a devastating effect on women's ability to work effectively or maintain personal relationships outside work. The Industrial Society survey (1993) showed that harassment at work can be one of the most upsetting, humiliating and destructive experiences that can happen to an employee. It interferes with thinking and judgement (37 per cent of cases), it makes it difficult to concentrate (18 per cent). Women who get harassed were less cooperative and productive (24 per cent), more prone to absences and lateness (5 per cent), behaviour changes and accidents (8 per cent). One in ten respondents reported leaving or transferring jobs or being denied career moves. In addition to this women experienced depression (8 per cent), sleep disturbances (7 per cent), confusion (8 per cent) and mood swings (7 per cent). Fewer than one in four said that harassment produced no changes in their work situation.

The Alfred Marks Bureau (1991) found that 68 per cent of those experiencing harassment felt humiliated or embarrassed by the experience. Among the harassers 42 per cent suffered no consequences and 21 per cent became angry or bad tempered. Of those who phoned the BBC help line in 1993, 33 out of 318 women left their job after harassment, many others retired early or took sick leave.

COHSE (1991) showed that 86 per cent of those experiencing sexual harassment said that it had had an adverse effect on their emotional well-being; 59 per cent said it had an adverse effect on their feelings towards work; 39 per cent said it had an adverse effect on their relationships with family, partners or friends; 33 per cent said that the quality of their work deteriorated and 20 per cent said it had an adverse effect on their physical health. Women commented: 'I was afraid to go to work', 'I had to retire on ill health', 'I left the NHS and now work for someone else'. Another 18 per cent said their performance was criticized, 18 per cent said their working conditions got worse and 10 per cent said they were denied promotion or training. In addition to this 10 per cent said that they, rather than the harasser, were transferred because of the incident.

In the Durham University study in 1992 effects reported included reduced concentration, anger, disgust, anxiety and loss of confidence. In the police survey (Her Majesty's Inspectorate of Constabulary 1993), one woman in ten had seriously considered leaving because of sexual harassment.

What action did those who were harassed take?

Surveys show that women have little faith in their employers doing anything about sexual harassment at work and therefore try to cope with the situation themselves. The Industrial Society (1993) found that about 30 per cent of women ignore it, 30 per cent make a joke of it and 30 per cent request an investigation. Telling the harasser to stop or threatening to report him had little effect or made things worse (in 44 per cent of cases), whereas strong action by the woman and the employer was very successful (in over 70 per cent of cases). Those who had used a grievance procedure tended to be from larger organizations (1000 to 2500 staff), which suggests that larger organizations have better established procedures that employees feel more confident about using.

According to the Alfred Marks survey (1991) most of those who experience harassment do nothing (71 per cent) or complain to a colleague (60 per cent). The survey showed that the most common reaction to harassment is to laugh it off (79 per cent), while 52 per cent resorted to emphatic verbal reaction and 19 per cent to physical rejection.

Of the people who called the BBC help line in 1993, many more women had tried to take action to stop the harassment than men. Men found that when they did complain, they were met with ridicule. Of the women 34 per cent confronted the harasser, 34 per cent complained to management, 24 per cent talked to colleagues, 13 per cent took legal action, 11 per cent went to their trade union, 7 per cent went to the police.

COHSE (1991) showed that more than a third of the women did not report the incident. Comments were along the lines of 'what's the point? No one listens'. Over half had reported the incidents, most of these did so verbally and informally. Of those who did report the incidents over half felt that they had not been dealt with appropriately. Comments included: 'No support from union at time of incident, nor from management', 'They shook their heads and laughed', 'He just laughed and said I shouldn't be so pretty'.

The Durham Survey (1992) showed that most students did not report cases of sexual harassment. Only 7 per cent reported incidents to college staff and 1 per cent to welfare officers.

Employers and sexual harassment

Sexual harassment is bad for business

Launching the Employment Department's guide on combating sexual harassment at work in 1992, which was sent to all employers within the UK with more than 10 staff, Robert Jackson, the employment minister, said: 'sexual harassment is bad for morale, bad for business efficiency and can cost employers money – through increased absenteeism, high staff turnover and having to deal with complaints' (*Equal Opportunities Review* 1992a: 6). Michael Rubenstein lists some of the personal effects of sexual harassment: anxiety, tension, irritability, depression, deterioration of personal relationships, hostility, inability to concentrate, sleeplessness, fatigue, headaches and other manifestations of stress (1992b: 10). Without proper procedures and a fully implemented sexual harassment policy, many women will not complain but take time off sick or leave.

The consequences of sexual harassment at work include disrupted work, reductions in productivity and quality of work, demoralized staff, financial loss related to increased turnover of staff. In the booklet *Statement on Harassment at Work*, the Institute of Personnel Management (1992: 4) says that

> No employer should underestimate the damage, tension and conflict within the workplace which harassment creates. The result is not just poor morale but higher labour turnover, reduced productivity, lower efficiency and divided teams. Although the effects may be difficult to quantify, they will eventually show through in the performance of the organisation.

Financial loss is a major consequence of sexual harassment. It is apparently 34 times more expensive to ignore the problem than to provide training (Wagner 1992). Legal costs can be high, although compensation at industrial tribunal has up until now been limited (see Chapter 3 on remedies under the Sex Discrimination Act), with many cases settled out of court. In 1992, the London Borough of Islington paid £15,000 in settlement of a case brought by a female trainee painter and decorator and in 1989 an advertising executive won £25,000 in an out of court settlement. Women Against Sexual Harassment (WASH) analysed 25 UK employers in 1992 (unpublished, reported verbally by WASH at the 'Sexual Harassment' Conference run by Industrial Relations Services in London in June 1992), calculating the financial consequences of their own sexual harassment cases including legal costs: the loss was between £5,000 for a relatively small incident to £265,857 for a complex case involving key staff. The cost of sexual harassment has also been calculated in the USA where the United States Merit System Protection Board's report *Sexual Harassment in the Federal Government* (1988) calculated that it cost the federal government $267 million dollars over a two year period (1985–86) in covering sick pay, reduced productivity and the loss of trained staff. Preventive measures are cheaper. Sexual harassment must be seen as a human resources issues. Women can take individual action but organizations taking corporate responsibility will be more effective.

Action taken by employers

Women's beliefs that employers are reluctant to take action is well founded as indeed surveys in this area show. Evidence indicates that managers' response to sexual harassment is poor. The most common punishment for someone found guilty of harassment is an official or unofficial warning (Davidson and Earnshaw 1991), the next most common action is to do nothing at all (49 per cent). In addition to this the victim was more likely to be relocated than the harasser.

The Alfred Marks survey (1991) showed that the most common outcome if an incident is reported is for the offender to be disciplined (43 per cent). However, in 32 per cent of cases being reported, the companies took no action.

The adoption of sexual harassment policies

An increasing number of companies are accepting their responsibilities and introducing sexual harassment policies. UK employers who have adopted sexual harassment policies include the

BBC, British Gas, Ford Motor Company, ICI, London Underground, National Westminster Bank, Royal Mail, Shell UK, ASDA stores as well as numerous local authorities. Public sector employers are more likely to have a sexual harassment policy than the private sector; 50 per cent of employers in the public sector have policies on sexual harassment compared to one employer out of five in the private sector (Industrial Relations Services survey, *Employment Trends* 1992). However, the pattern is changing as more private sector employers are adopting policies.

The study by the Manchester School of Management (Davidson and Earnshaw 1991) showed that 88 per cent of personnel directors had not issued a policy statement of any kind. Of those who had, 93 per cent had done so without consultation with the union (this issue will be taken up in Chapter 6) and 92 per cent had never consulted the union on any issue to do with sexual harassment. Of those who had policies only 21 per cent gave training to those responsible for implementing the policy (this issue will be picked up in Chapter 7). Only 32 per cent of those who had issued policies had procedures for dealing with sexual harassment in the grievance and disciplinary procedures as well as a sexual harassment policy.

In 1993, an Industrial Society survey showed that, overall, 40 per cent of employers in Britain have sexual harassment policies. This is approximately half the number in the United States (Industrial Society Survey 1993:xxix). Of the people they surveyed 30 per cent said they did not have a policy and 22 per cent said that they did not know whether their organization had one or not. This probably means that some organizations do have policies but have not publicized them.

Although many organizations do not yet have sexual harassment policies, most are aware that cases get reported; of 132 employers surveyed by the Industrial Relations Services (*Employment Trends* 1992) over half said that cases of sexual harassment had been reported. In addition to this nearly all organizations are aware of the potential unlawfulness of sexual harassment at work, but fewer are aware of their own legal obligations: the study from the Manchester School of Management showed that 93 per cent of organizations were aware that sexual harassment was potentially unlawful under the Sex Discrimination Act, yet only 74 per cent of personnel managers surveyed knew that the employer was liable for sexual harassment perpetrated by their employees (Davidson and Earnshaw1991: 17). The research also showed that 65 per cent of employers accepted that sexual harassment was a serious management issue.

Conclusion

This chapter has given a definition of sexual harassment, shown the extent to which it occurs and argued that ignoring sexual harassment does not make good business sense. The chapter has given no explanation of why it occurs. An understanding of sexual harassment is crucial if employers and others concerned about sexual harassment wish to tackle it successfully. We know from the surveys that sexual harassment is linked to power; harassers tend to be those in positions of authority, abusing this power. As said earlier in this chapter, this is a difference between sexual harassment and other forms of sexual behaviour; a student who repeatedly asks her tutor for dates can be extremely annoying, whereas a tutor who repeatedly asks a student for dates is threatening because he has the power to affect her life. The next chapter takes a close look at women's experiences of sexual harassment and particularly analyses the power game inherent in sexual harassment.

2

SEXISM AND SEXUAL HARASSMENT

Sexual harassment is unwanted, uninvited and unwelcome behaviour based on gender. A crucial component of the definition of sexual harassment is the effect of the behaviour on the recipient. The harasser's intention is one thing – the effect of his behaviour on the woman is another. The two are not necessarily related, a harasser may not directly intend to offend and yet be offensive. Nevertheless it is important to know why men harass women since such understanding can be used to help prevent harassment.

This chapter aims to give sexual harassment a theoretical framework. It looks at the impact of sexual harassment through women's perceptions, and outlines what sexual harassment is really about and what harassers are attempting to achieve by such behaviour. Finally the importance of equal opportunities policies are examined as they provide a background against which an organization can start to tackle sexual harassment at work.

A view from the inside: women's experiences of sexual harassment

This section looks at the impact of sexual harassment on women from their initial feelings of bewilderment to their loss of identity.

18

It explores through these experiences how sexual harassment is felt by women as a gender based power game rather than anything to do with sex. Much of this section is based on my experience at City Centre where I advise women who have been sexually harassed. Many of the quotations come from a study in which I undertook in-depth interviews with women who had been harassed (Collier 1993). City Centre is a London based advice agency which deals with employment issues as they affect office workers. Requests for advice on sexual harassment have risen sharply over the last three years.

A bewildering experience

Typically, women experiencing sexual harassment feel utterly confused at what is happening. When harassment begins there is a feeling of unreality. Women invariably ask themselves 'Is this really happening?' Even when it becomes obvious something is happening to them women still feel confused and bewildered by the experience. Women repeat again and again 'Why me?' and more commonly, 'I don't really understand what is going on'. Many of the women who phone up to ask for advice start by saying 'I am not sure if I am imagining it' or 'I don't know if this is a lot of fuss about nothing but . . .' Often they find it difficult putting a name to what is going on, for few immediately identify it as sexual harassment. One young woman who was on a Youth Training Scheme in an office phoned saying 'Maybe this is nothing but I feel so worried about going to work, my boss leans right over the table towards me whenever he speaks to me, coming really close to me'.

Another woman said that at first she thought the communication problems between her and her boss were just a management problem, his behaviour seemed 'simply weird'. He would sometimes shout and be abusive and the next instant become perfectly calm and reasonably pleasant. One minute he would ignore her, then he would do something to draw everyone's attention to her. On one occasion he kept her standing in the office doorway after having asked to see her, and then he turned around, looked her carefully up and down and said to the other men in the office 'Doesn't she look nice, she does take a lot of care

19

of her appearance don't you think?' This woman commented 'I had the instinctive and strong feeling that it was wrong but I didn't know it was sexual harassment. I thought sexual harassment was about flirtatious secretaries in tight blouses'.

Women generally feel threatened, confused but not quite sure whether they are justified in their feelings and not sure why they have these feelings. One woman began to feel she was *bad*, that there must be something wrong with her because she couldn't make sense of the situation. She had refused to answer personal questions about her private life ('What perfume do you use?', 'What soap do you use?'), had complained about personal remarks ('I don't like your smell') and refused to do personal favours to her boss (massage his shoulder). After this he became sarcastic and made derogatory remarks about her work. She had not at first connected her refusals and complaints with his increasingly disagreeable behaviour. She had not thought of sexual harassment or recognized the victimization to which she was being subjected. All she felt was that something was wrong with her, but she couldn't work out what. She felt uneasy and confused.

Another woman, a student, also felt bewildered by her tutor's attitude. First he praised her work, then he repeatedly accused her of being 'over ambitious' saying 'I have met your type before'. At the same time as he criticized her work, he gave her good grades. At the same time as he made critical remarks about her as a person, he invited her to meet him outside college. When she refused he became spiteful; he said she was 'difficult to teach'. The experience was confusing but also frightening as his behaviour was somewhat mysterious: he showed her postcards, one depicting medieval scenes of Hell (with a Latin inscription saying 'The lustful will be punished') and the other the inside of a church on the back of which he had written 'You were there' (which he knew was untrue). He phoned her at home, and again the conversation was ambiguous. After she had made it clear she did not want a sexual relationship with him he answered that he didn't want to have sex with her (adding that he could have easy sex any time), but he also said that when he spoke to her on the phone it felt like 'making love to her'. On one occasion on the phone he said to her 'Don't hurt me any more' (this was confusing to her; he was the one who was upsetting her!) and 'Tell me you feel warm towards me'. Such double messages confounded her sense of confusion. All these experiences add to the feelings of bewilderment and illustrate the difficulty women have in understanding what is happening to them.

Another woman felt thrown when the man she was working for called her into the office and said quite unexpectedly: 'You are everything I would want in a woman, I can't fault your work but I am a married man and you would stand in the way of my career'. She was told not to return to work after Christmas. She felt shaken and speechless, 'I just didn't know what to say to him'. She had never gone out with him, never had a drink with him and he had never made personal advances to her. His behaviour seemed incomprehensible.

Whether it involves looks, talk or touching, women's initial response to sexual harassment is one of shock and disbelief. They feel that there must be some misunderstanding. Women will often try to ignore it as if it must have been a mistake. Even if you know all about sexual harassment it still comes as a shock. Terry Pattinson recounts how Brenda Dean, General Secretary of the Society of Graphical and Allied Trades (SOGAT), was sitting at a table when the man next to her started fondling her thigh. She was so amazed anyone would have the nerve, she could not think of what else to do but ignore it (Pattinson, 1991:41). Sexual harassment behaviours are confusing and frightening because 'they represent an unwanted and unsought intrusion by men into women's feelings, thoughts, behaviours, space, time, energies and bodies' (Wise and Stanley 1987:71). One woman described how her boss would sit very close to her, just touching her, reading the letters she had typed on her computer. She would feel a mixture of 'anger, embarrassment and humiliation'. When she asked him not to sit so close he complained that she was being difficult. When she complained to his manager, her boss accused her of gossiping. She knew something was wrong with his behaviour but didn't quite know what or whether she was justified in feeling uncomfortable about it. She felt increasingly panic-stricken and sick.

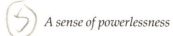 *A sense of powerlessness*

Sexual harassment is often difficult for women to name; it often becomes part of the accepted office environment, it is sufficiently pervasive . . . as to be nearly invisible. Contained by internalized and structural forms of power, it has been nearly inaudible . . . Tacitly, it has been both acceptable and taboo; acceptable for men to do, taboo for women to confront, even to themselves.

(MacKinnon 1979: 1)

Wise and Stanley refer to sexual harassment as 'the dripping tap' because 'most sexual harassment is . . . small, mundane and accumulating' (1987: 114).

Throughout their experiences of sexual harassment women feel powerless. Many women talk of being 'stunned' or 'speechless' when facing sexual harassment. Susie Orbach (1991) compares women who have experienced sexual harassment in this respect to children who have experienced sexual abuse:

that silence is the silence of the powerless victim who feels and knows something is wrong but who has no one to turn to; who has no words to speak that can communicate the hurt, the wrong, the mistreatment; who has little hope that the situation will change.

The experience can be so painful that women will often deny it is happening or play down the severity of the incidents. Naming the behaviour as sexual harassment can be a powerful experience for women that gives them some sense of control over the situation.

Women who are being sexually harassed feel they are powerless, they feel that something is happening which is beyond their control. They are made to feel small and threatened. 'He just sat and stared at me' or 'He would scream invectives and obscenities at me', 'He treated me like a dog' are typical of the things women say. One woman had her boss demanding she come out of the toilet immediately, she hurried out assuming it was something urgent only to hear him say 'Oh, it was nothing, never mind'. Another woman said 'What frightened me was the power he had, he made it clear that my career was in his hands'. A student said: 'I felt paralysed by fear of offending someone who had so much power over my future and aspirations'.

The manager of one woman used to have all the women in the

office (200 to 300 of them) together for a meeting and say to them 'when you sign in to say you are sick I want you to tell me if it is menstruating pains'. This sort of intrusion into women's private lives is part of the power game which undermines women's confidence and keeps them in their place; as one woman said:

> It is the same feeling as if you got up one morning, started getting dressed then noticed that your curtains were not drawn and a man was watching you – it is that sort of intrusion. You end up feeling like crossing your legs whenever you are sitting on a chair and folding your arms to hide your breasts. I wish I could get back my self-esteem and feel good about myself again.

These experiences tally with surveys on sexual harassment which show that the most common reaction to sexual harassment is 'embarrassment' and 'humiliation' (Alfred Marks Bureau 1991). This is followed by other reactions such as feeling 'tense, emotional, unable to concentrate'.

Loss of identity

The sense of confusion women feel in sexual harassment is accompanied by a loss of privacy and a loss of identity. One woman described how her boss phoned her up at home to talk about work. She was about to have a bath so said she would phone him back later. After her bath she called him back as arranged. Although she phoned about work, he kept asking personal questions about her bathing habits. She did not know that he had several male members of staff in his office who all listened to what she was saying, but this fact compounded her feeling of loss of privacy when she found out the next day. She was speechless and didn't know how to react; 'It goes right to your core . . . it is so intimate . . . it is so much what you are about as a woman'. Later, at her court hearing he said she was 'hysterical, a liar, not up to the job, you know what women are like'. This same man would search through her desk when she was not at the office. He abused her verbally on a regular basis; 'I felt violated'. Finally he threatened her physically. She resigned and brought a charge for assault against him as well as taking a sexual harassment case to an industrial tribunal. All during the time she worked, she had wondered 'What is wrong with me? What is it about me that makes him do this? Why am I so horrible?' She was still asking herself that question two years later; 'There is still a part of me that needs to make sense of it . . . Why? What is it in me?. . . You always come back to questioning yourself'. She says: 'I tried to wear pastel colours that would make me disappear, I also got very fat. I wanted people to like me'.

I have already mentioned how one man insisted his secretary come out of the toilet for no reason at all. This same man also persisted in asking her what soap or cologne she used. He ordered her to massage his shoulder. When she did he made satisfied groans of a sexual nature. When she refused to massage him any more he said: 'But you are Japanese, all Japanese women service their bosses in this way'. She still refused, pointing out that his assumptions about Japanese women were not true. He then became vindictive. He claimed her smell gave him a headache, a comment designed to give him power over her as a woman and as non-white (he himself was white). He was making it clear to her that she was 'a problem' to him on both counts. He would do all these things in front of other male members of staff. She felt ashamed, insulted, scared and vulnerable. She felt he had invaded her privacy and even her 'person'. Eventually he sacked her. She felt she had done something wrong and she lost faith in herself as a worker, a wife and a mother. She could not make sense of what was happening. All this was happening to a woman who described herself as neither young nor pretty, middle aged, happily married with several children.

The student mentioned earlier felt at a loss when her tutor phoned her up to talk about her work, but while she persisted in discussing her work he kept making personal comments disregarding what she was saying about her work. She felt his remarks as 'invasive'.

One woman, who refused to take any notice of her boss's amorous remarks and who eventually lost her job (but won her case at industrial tribunal), said

> I like working with men, this was nothing to do with that. It wasn't that he ever even touched me. It was much deeper

than that and much more complicated, much more hurtful. If he had touched me I could have handled that. It was as if he said to himself: 'she has turned me down, I will finish her' and he did.

He stopped all her chances of promotion and eventually ensured she got no more work. She did not have a contract with the company; she was placed there by an agency who regularly found her work with this same organization. Mysteriously the agency found her no more work after her case, 'It makes you wonder, should you complain . . . should I have just sat back and let them walk all over me . . . it was as if I was being manipulated by all these people to suit them'. Even after her case was won she felt she had lost her sense of self:

Sexual harassment isn't about touching, it goes much deeper. People I used to work with don't want to be seen with me. You feel isolated, as if you are in quarantine . . . I don't know . . . I keep thinking I could go back to work normally, but I don't know . . . people don't know what you go through, your life is taken over . . . Unless you have been through it yourself, it is very difficult to explain . . . very difficult to put into words. You feel mentally raped.

The impact on women's health

Most women who have been sexually harassed experience mental and physical health problems. This is true whether they complain about it or keep quiet. The most common mental problem is lack of concentration: 'My ability to concentrate became very difficult, I was immobilized, at home too, I loved to cook but I would cut my fingers . . . I couldn't sit and read a book'. Other common symptoms include headaches, nausea, sleeplessness (many women need medication to sleep as a result of their experiences), anorexia, overeating and allergic reactions such as eczema. Palpitations and panic attacks are also common. One woman described how she went shopping, then after putting all her goods into carrier bags she just froze, she couldn't move, she was panic-stricken and had to sit with her bags by the till. Another time, the same woman had to stop driving after a particular incident of harassment as she 'just could not breathe'. Terry Pattinson describes a woman who needed 'medical treatment as a result of her experiences. Depression was one illness brought about by the harassment she had suffered and she had lost three stone in weight' (1991: 107). The *Evening Standard* quoted a case of a woman who had been sexually harassed by two men who made comments about her legs and lewd sexual suggestions:

> I was so worried about the case in the months up to it I went off sex. I simply couldn't be intimate with my husband. I would cry easily and argue all the time. He said I didn't laugh like I used to . . . My children suffered during the whole episode. They would say 'Why is mummy being grumpy, why is she snapping?'
>
> (*Evening Standard*, 15 October 1991, p. 23)

Loss of libido is something all women mention.

The symptoms continue in some cases for many years. The student, quoted above, met her tutor again some time after her studies had finished and after she had ceased to have contact with him, yet she felt 'sick and shaky' and had to leave the room. The ordeal of making a complaint or going through an industrial tribunal can exacerbate the symptoms. One woman said of the whole experience: 'I was just dying inside, but kept going one day at a time'. Another compared it to drowning saying: 'It is like learning to swim, I have been thrown in the deep end and left there', She continued:

> It has been two years now, I am not getting any better, I am beginning to question things, even my friends. I still get panic attacks, I don't want to be left alone. I have changed, I used to be part of any mischief going. Now I just want to stay at home, I just wait for every day to come.

Sexism and sexual harassment

This section analyses the reasons why sexual harassment occurs and the environment in which it occurs.

Sexism and sexual harassment

Sexual harassment is about power

A common assumption is that sexual harassment is about flirtation or about sex. However, most writers agree that it is about neither of these:

> The major change concerns whether sexual harassment is to be seen as harassment which uses sex (among other things) in order to accomplish power, or as harassment which uses power in order to get sex. The fundamental issue here then is whether we should understand sexual harassment as a power behaviour or as a sexual behaviour.
>
> (Wise and Stanley 1987: 53).

From the previous section on women's experiences, it becomes evident that sexual harassment is about power.

Men are invariably in positions of seniority at work, but quite independently of work, men have power because of their position in society. Most of the time sexual harassment occurs when men abuse the power they have over women. Women are seen as 'available' to men and in a sense there *for* men; this is particularly true of some groups of women such as black women. Black women, because of the history of slavery when people were literally owned by others, are seen as more 'available', more open to abuse.

Sexual harassment is used as a means of maintaining power. Terry Pattinson (1991: 138) quotes Diana Lamplugh:

> 'the traditional male roles – father, husband, lover – are useful to men in the workplace because they help men to control women. Men will 'flirt' with female subordinates, for example, in order to make it difficult for them to ask for rises or to refuse to do work that is outside their job description'.

Managers routinely use sexual harassment whether in jest or in abuse as means of maintaining authority (Pringle 1988: 94). Sue Wise and Liz Stanley write: 'sexual harassment may sometimes involve "sexual" behaviours of one kind or another, but this "sexual" is the means to an end and not an end in itself. Power is the desired element involved; and females and sex are merely means of enabling them to do 'power' (1987: 64). Much of what was previously described in this chapter is an abuse of power.

27

Many of the harassers are described by women as abusing their power in this way: 'His management style was to manage by fear', 'He was a control freak'; this seemed to be particularly true if women were seen to be 'too assertive' or 'too powerful'. A student may be encouraged by her tutor in her work until she gets an 'A' for an essay, then be criticized by the tutor with goading remarks such as 'why do you have to work so hard?'. A student to whom this happened felt that the tutor's comments were calculated to crush any effort she made: 'by doing well I felt he thought I was threatening his masculinity, I couldn't understand why'. Wise and Stanley (1987: 189) understand this behaviour: 'Men have ways of dealing with uppity women who they think have power . . . one of the main ways is to de-threaten such women by sexualising them'. Sexual harassment, in following a pattern of intrusion into women's lives, 'is a form of policing' (Wise and Stanley, 1987: 15). Typical behaviour meted out by managers includes throwing work at the woman's face (this has been reported to me on many occasions), tearing work up, giving unrealistic deadlines, staring, verbal abuse, stroking bottoms or breasts, demanding personal details about women's lives, locking the door of the office when women are called into a meeting with him, unwanted kissing on the cheeks, asking for a massage and threatened assault or attempted rape. These are all ways of trying to control women by abusing power.

Such behaviour may start in the classroom where boys try to exert control over girls through bullying and language: 'In many classrooms about Britain boys call girls 'slags', 'tarts', 'sluts', 'dogs', 'cows' and 'bitches' for no other reason than that of intimidation' (Herbert 1992: 81). This intimidation is a means of gaining power.

Women depersonalized

Sexual harassment at work is an extension of sexual harassment in everyday life with the difference that at work women are seen as intruders in the workplace. Women do not belong to the workplace in the same way as men do. The other crucial difference is that sexual harassment at work is potentially unlawful. Apart from rape or physical assault, no legislation protects women against everyday harassment. However, to understand sexual harassment at work, it is important to have an understanding of sexual harassment in everyday life.

Through sexual harassment women are made to feel that they cannot be themselves and that in a sense they are there for men. Many writers have analysed the way in which women are made to feel they are 'other'. If women are non-white they are 'other/other'. This was certainly the case with the Japanese woman quoted earlier who was made to feel she was not just a worker but 'a woman' and 'Japanese', 'other' on two counts. The same is felt by women who are lesbians.

Society makes women what they are, as Simone de Beauvoir makes clear in the opening sentence of *The Second Sex* (1949): 'One is not born, rather one becomes a woman'. Part of this 'otherness' means that women are not just 'non-men' but they also are made to feel that they are expected to support and reflect men and particularly men's power. Rosi Braidotti says: 'Woman was constituted and produced by established social norms which made her into man's eternal mirror' (1991: 127). This is similar to Virginia Woolf who writes: 'Women have served all these centuries as looking glasses possessing the magic and delicious power of reflecting the figure of man at twice its natural size' (1929: 33). Sue Wise and Liz Stanley quote Woolf adding:

> the purpose is to reduce women to objects of men's whims and wishes and so to enhance men's perceptions of themselves: it is in effect, as Virginia Woolf so acutely pointed out, a way of these men looking into a symbolic mirror which reflects them as gigantically powerful.
>
> (1987: 80)

In referring to Virginia Woolf, Rosi Braidotti also quotes Kate Millett (1973) who says that patriarchy is the space inside which the subject is constituted; Braidotti continues this theme saying that 'the setting up of the male subject as the measure of all things requires the positing of the woman as other-than, that is to say less-than, and subordinate to the point of reference' (1991: 177). Wise and Stanley make a similar point when they say: 'male reality, or, as we previously called it, sexist reality, involves a belief system whereby men and what men think and do constitutes "the norm"'(1987: 81).

This is part of why women feel, in sexual harassment, that something is happening which is nothing to do with them. Indeed it isn't, it is something in which men are involved. Sexual harassment is another example of women being treated as objects for men; it is an experience which like other experiences women have 'denies their *entitlement* to subjectivity' (Braidotti 1991: 264). One reason why it is so painful for women is that it reminds them that in a sense they have no reality. Whatever women are, however good they are at their work they are first and foremost women and as such objects for men. Sexual harassment ensures that they don't forget it, 'to be a woman is to have "woman" as your "master status", regardless of whether you are also a brain surgeon or a welder or a housewife' (Wise and Stanley, 1987: 58).

All this adds to the feeling that in sexual harassment women lose privacy; they lose the sense of who they are since they just become 'woman' in the sense in which 'woman' is determined by men, that is, something for someone else, something 'public'. As one woman told me: 'it goes right to your core . . . it is so much what you are about as a woman'. This feeling comes out too when women feel they are being 'undressed' by a man's gaze. Jean-Paul Sartre understood such feelings well though he did not analyse them in terms of male/female relations; that was done later by Simone de Beauvoir. In *Being and Nothingness*, Sartre talks about the way in which other people can 'set the parameters of my world by fixing their gaze on me', it is as if suddenly something has appeared 'which has stolen my world . . . the appearance of other beings in the world corresponds to the whole universe slowly sliding away' (1943: 313). Sartre adds that 'through other people looking at me, I experience myself as fixed in the middle of the world, as if in danger' (1943: 327) (my translations). This is exactly the way women have felt transfixed by the experience ('I was stunned, speechless', 'I couldn't move'), 'in danger' because the experience was not of their making and their being itself was under threat. As Sartre says, seeing one's body as an object through someone else's eyes is an experience of alienation, it is as if my body is no longer mine, it is a denial of my right as a human being. The woman who described sexual harassment as being similar to the experience of being watched by a peeping Tom was expressing the same view. The most obvious example of this is when men undress a woman with their eyes.

Sexual harassment is in this same sense an attempt at possessing a person as an object, 'a woman' and not as 'a person'. What might appear to be a relatively unimportant level of harassment is just as powerful in this respect as 'serious' physical harassment such as attempted rape. In this context, Elizabeth Stanko (1988: 92) quotes the case of a police woman who arrived at work one day to find 'a photograph of her head pasted to a pornographic picture and posted throughout the police station. At this point, her gender, her sexual being, was the focus of attention, not her work performance.' It is a way of neutralizing someone, of denying their humanity, their personhood. This is echoed in many of the things women have said: 'he felt I was too good', 'too powerful', 'he wanted to cut me down to size' etc. The harasser often acts as if the woman is doing something awful to him!

Simone de Beauvoir saw very clearly how this process develops. A girl, she says 'is taught that to please she must try to please, she must make herself object; she should therefore renounce her autonomy' (1949: 20). She continues:

it is a strange experience for an individual who feels himself to be an autonomous and transcendent subject, an absolute, to discover inferiority in himself as a fixed and preordained essence: it is a strange experience for whoever regards himself as the One to be revealed to himself as otherness, alterity. This is what happens to the little girl when doing her apprenticeship for life in the world, she grasps what it means to be a woman therein.

(1949: 35)

The pain of sexual harassment is partly due to the realization that however much you achieve in work or study, however much you affirm yourself as an autonomous person, society in the form of the harasser will remind you that your destiny is not yours. As de Beauvoir says:

the advantage man enjoys, which makes itself felt from his childhood, is that his vocation as a human being in no way runs counter to his destiny as a male . . . he is not divided, whereas it is required of woman that in order to realize her femininity she must make herself object and prey, which is to say that she must renounce her claims as sovereign subject.

(1949: 374)

The extent to which women don't count as subjects is also illustrated by the comment made by British Rail after a train driver was sacked for sexually harassing a member of staff: 'he had to be sacked because his behaviour was putting passengers in danger' (forget about what it was doing to the woman!). A not dissimilar attitude to women was displayed in an article in the *British Medical Journal* in 1991 (see Collier and Collier 1991). The article was about the rape of women in former Yugoslavia and the authors concluded that it was a terrible experience for the husband who had to watch. No mention was made of the effect on the women.

As has been said many times, sexual harassment is not about flirtation or attempts at seduction. The difference between sexual harassment and flirtation is that in sexual harassment the other person is being treated as an object (an 'other'), whereas in flirtation (where both partners engage in the behaviour) the other person is being treated as a person (not merely as a 'woman'). Women have learnt to recognize the language of flirtation and do not confuse them. Flirtation might make a women feel flattered, harassment always makes her feel denigrated.

Sexual harassment is a form of sexism

Many harassers behave in a typically sexist way in general; 'he treated all women with utter contempt', 'his whole attitude towards women in the office was "just flutter your eyelids and people will say yes"', 'women just have to uncross their legs to get what they want' and so on. Sexual harassment flourishes within the everyday sexism women experience at work. Much of this is accepted by all, as one woman said: 'if ever I write a book about my experience I shall call it *Socially Acceptable Conduct* since everything he did to me, he claimed at the tribunal, fell within socially acceptable conduct'.

Sexual harassment is used to keep women out of what is seen as a male preserve and for this reason it is a form of discrimination against women. Keeping women in segregated jobs (which incidentally are usually jobs which service men: clerical, cleaning, cooking, caring jobs) is also sex discrimination. The caring and servicing roles that women fulfil at home are also the ones they are expected to play at work. The secretary thus becomes an office 'wife'. The financial dependence of women on men is replicated from the home to the workplace. Men use sexual harassment and their power to reinforce sexist attitudes at work:

> Sexuality can be used as a power tool for those in positions of authority, and because males are more often found in such positions in the workplace, men tend to exploit women sexually as a means to keep them in subordinate positions and to limit the access women have to good jobs.
>
> (DiTomaso 1989: 73)

Although referring to everyday life rather than the workplace, Wise and Stanley make the same point when they say:

> Sexual harassment therefore serves to keep women, and men, in our respective places: the places that men define as appropriate; and it also, of course, serves so as to bring back into line, by force if necessary, any woman who departs from this or who doesn't fit in with how she's supposed to be.
>
> (1987: 82)

Wise and Stanley also point out that since such behaviour is not about sexuality but about power, gay men are just as likely to be sexist as heterosexual men (1987: 91).

Sexual harassment therefore plays an important role in society: maintaining a status quo. Women learn to accept it and are expected to put up with it. Women find that if they object to this behaviour the chances are that it will escalate which is why most women suffer in silence. Women even act as accomplices to this sexism. Elizabeth Stanko (1988: 93) describes this acceptance by saying: 'Her work context includes a previously hidden part of the job description; the employee must be willing to field any and all sexual advances, wanted and unwanted'. In many occupations women are expected to appear 'attractive' (to men), for example barmaids and secretaries; it is part of the job requirement to such an extent that 'being female, in women's work, may in fact be a "set-up" for harassment' (Stanko, 1988: 95).

Women regularly complain at how often men act as if the women in the office are there 'for the men', they 'seem to be under some impression that they're as available as the morning coffee' (Read 1982: 57). All this is part of the power game which keeps women in their place. It is ironic that 'dressing the part' is expected of women in many jobs whilst at the same time if they are harassed they are often blamed for it with comments such as 'well, what do you expect dressed in that short skirt'. Terry Pattinson maintains that women can provoke sexual harassment. He says one might 'point out that a man carrying one million pounds in a suitcase at midnight in a Glasgow side street does not deserve to be mugged . . . but . . . "were you not tempting fate?" the police, the insurance company and the bank manager might ask'. He continues: 'The same question, in my opinion, could legitimately be put to a woman dressing and behaving like Jodie Foster' (1991: 26). This argument is flawed, both men and women run the same risk if they carry a suitcase full of money. On the other hand men run little risk of sexual harassment however they choose to dress, there is no equality here. And of course dressing in a particular way does not give anyone the right to tease or harass. To say that it does justify harassment would be like saying to a male Sikh that he should expect racist comments if he wears a turban. Both these types of behaviour are a symptom of shifting the blame away from where it belongs and 'blaming the victim'.

Sexual harassment is sex discrimination as it undercuts women's equality at work. Much of it is part of ordinary everyday sexism whereby women are put down and thus excluded from areas of work. Within sexist behaviour, sexual harassment is, as has been said before, behaviour which is unwanted by the recipient. A lot of everyday sexism, for example patronizing language, is simply ignored or so common as to be 'invisible'. Sexual harassment is a form of sexism, but not all sexism is sexual harassment. Sedley and Benn try to distinguish the two:

It is very difficult to draw the line between sexism at work and sexual harassment, but an arbitrary line may have to be drawn when we are thinking about effective remedies. They are part of the same phenomenon, but sexual harassment is more direct and personal.

(1982: 8)

Male dominated environments

Sexual harassment is more likely to occur in male-dominated environments. A study done by Leeds Trade Union and Community Resource and Information Centre (TUCRIC) in 1983 showed that 96 per cent of women working in traditional male environments were harassed compared with 48 per cent working in non-male environments. Nancy DiTomaso (1989) surveyed the experiences of 360 workers in three traditional male organizations: a heavy manufacturing firm, a service firm and a public agency. Women working in these industries experienced extremely unpleasant working conditions. The behaviour of the men was not ordinary male/female behaviour, it was not flirtatious, it was offensive: 'Women were not treated as co-workers, but as women *per se*. Sexuality became part of the workplace negotiations' (1989: 85). Women felt men were hostile to them whilst at the same time making demands on them. It seems that women who appear to challenge men by 'taking their jobs' are more likely to face sexual harassment. It is as if 'by entering the job market women place themselves in competition with men, who then attempt, if they have the power, to secure their dominant roles by emphasising the "womanness" of their female co-workers' (1989: 88). DiTomaso points out that men can humiliate women by making public something which should be private (sexual advances). Men who display their sexuality in public are seen to be displaying their manhood, women on the other hand, who display their sexuality in public are seen as degrading themselves or 'asking for trouble'.

As previously discussed, a survey of the police showed very high levels of sexual harassment (Her Majesty's Inspectorate of Constabulary 1993). Nine out of ten women officers experienced sexual harassment at work. From the men's point of view the

35

speculation some men, see as such. But becoming old fashioned. Less towards more sensitive to women

atmosphere is one of jovial fun, but in reality this is at the expense of women. Elizabeth Stanko also analyses the way women are treated in male dominated environments and concludes: 'Women, it is commonly assumed, by entering into men's territory, must expect and accept these displays of healthy male heterosexuality' (1988: 97). One woman who contacted City Centre worked in a sorting office where there were 50 men and two women. The daily banter and sexual innuendos concentrated increasingly on her. Her children were grown up and she cared for a disabled husband. The men's assumption was that she could not possibly be 'getting enough of it'. When she complained about their behaviour they changed their banter to hate messages. When she entered the room they all repeatedly chanted the letters H–A–T–E followed by her own initials H–N–B. This was repeated again and again till the chant died down. This type of behaviour may be seen as 'harmless to men and important to the construction of their working environment. From a male point of view, the harmful effects of sexual harassment are not understood as intrusions, just male "fun"' (Stanko 1988: 97).

Several authors have analysed this 'compulsory heterosexuality' (Rich, Hearn and Parkin and Pringle): 'It involves the domination of men's heterosexuality over women's heterosexuality and the subordination of all other forms of sexuality' (Pringle 1988: 94). In her research on secretaries, Rosemary Pringle found that very few lesbians dared to be 'out' and that those who were 'out' in the office were seen as the 'tame pervert' (1988: 95). Pringle also argues that 'sexual harassment functions particularly to keep women out of non-traditional occupations and to reinforce their secondary status in the workplace' (1988: 93). She gives an example of a male firm of solicitors where sexual banter was rife with much fondling and 'patting of bottoms'. In this firm people also enjoyed a common social life and intermarried. Ex-secretaries brought their babies to work for visits. But beneath this 'enforced egalitarianism and informality there was a rigidly enforced sexual division of labour. The partners could not imagine taking on a woman lawyer or the possibility that any of the "girls" might have the capacity to do law' (1988: 93).

Sexual harassment and equal opportunities

In organizations which do not have clear policies on women's equality, women are more likely to experience sexual harassment since, as we have just seen, sexism is more likely to prevail. Sexual harassment is likely to exist wherever the unequal distribution of power between men and women is greatest. Any harassment policy should therefore be linked to a policy which aims to redress this inequality. It should be part of an equal opportunities policy. This is the advice given in the European Commission's guide on sexual harassment: 'Sexual harassment policies will be more effective when linked with broader equal opportunities policies geared towards improving the overall position of women in the organisation' (1993: 34). The introduction of an equal opportunities policy will involve an organization in self-examination as it will reveal where inequalities exist and how power is exercised in the workplace. For example it will show how people are appointed, trained and promoted and whether these processes are discriminatory and who has the power of decision in each of these cases. In introducing a sexual harassment policy any organization will be even more tested as to its whole attitude towards women. This is why it is best to tackle 'attitudes towards women' first and to have systems in place which address equality generally before starting to address sexual harassment.

Many everyday sexist attitudes that women encounter at work rely on myths about women: women don't want a career, women work for pin money, women can't do men's work, women lack ambition, women returners have acquired no skills since leaving work, women do not make good managers, it is not worth women having a career as they will leave to have children. Such myths stand in the way of women achieving equality at work. An equal opportunities policy is evidence of an employer's commitment to countering the myths that exist around women and work.

An equal opportunities policy should cover discrimination in advertising, recruitment, training and promotion. Guidelines on these are available from the Equal Opportunities Commission (EOC) and the Institute of Personnel Management. A good equal opportunities policy will look at all areas where there may be discrimination. It will also compensate for the disadvantages faced by certain groups of people by implementing a programme of positive action – which is allowed under the law. Positive action is not the same as positive discrimination. Positive discrimination would be giving preference to women over men in job applications even if men are better qualified. This is illegal. Positive action is providing the means which will enable women to become as able as men to compete for jobs. This can be done by providing specialist training for certain groups of people under-represented in a particular part of the workforce. Women can also be helped by providing a crèche, good maternity arrangements, dependency leave, career breaks and so on. Finally, a good policy will tackle organizational discrimination by providing training for managers and by examining the current managerial practices operating within the organization which may have a discrimi-natory bias. Any organization implementing an equal opportuni-ties policy should introduce monitoring. Without this it will be impossible to tell where the organization is and where it needs to go; it will also be impossible to measure any progress being made. Successful implementation requires commitment and drive from the top (see Wilkinson 1992).

Ideally an equal opportunities policy should have a policy statement publicly supported by top management, should cover all forms of discrimination (for example discrimination on the grounds of gender, race, age, disability, sexuality, HIV/AIDS status, each being considered separately). The policy should be publicized continuously to the whole workforce as well as to applicants, consulted upon with the trade unions and regularly monitored.

The following is an extract from Ford's Equal Opportunities Statement, jointly signed by the company and its trade union:

The company will ensure that individuals are recruited and selected, promoted and treated on objective criteria having regard to relevant aptitudes, potential, skills and abilities. In particular, no applicant or employee will be placed at a disadvantage by requirements or conditions which are not necessary to the performance of the job or which constitute indirect unfair discrimination . . . opportunities will be taken, through language, images or declarations, as appropriate, to show that the company is an equal opportunity employer.

An example of an equal opportunities policy is given in Appendix 1.

Conclusion

Sexual harassment has a profound effect on women, threatening their sense of identity and making it extremely difficult to return to employment or study with any confidence. There is a clear link between the way women experience sexual harassment and the power game played by the harasser. The harasser attempts to enhance his position of superiority by actions which destroy a woman's sense of identity. As Rosemary Pringle says 'it is ironic that women are perceived as using sex to their advantage. They are much less likely to initiate sexual encounters and more likely to be hurt by sex at work' (1988: 94). Sexual harassment is a power game which results in women's vulnerability and inferiority being emphasized.

It is part of the general sexism that prevails in society which is why harassment of men by women has a different meaning from harassment of women by men. Although men can experience harassment from women, they do not experience it as discrimination. On the whole men report feeling 'flattered' by women's advances whereas women do not (Pringle 1988: 94). Harassment of women is linked to a wider picture of how women are treated generally in society: 'When a man does a particular piece of behaviour, say "compliments" a woman on the way she looks – it means something very different from the apparently "same" behaviour done by a woman to a man' (Wise and Stanley 1987: 66).

Sexual harassment is a barrier to women's personal development at work. It is therefore crucial for any organization without a full equal opportunities policy to adopt one if there is any real intention of preventing sexual harassment.

Chapter 1 outlined the financial reasons for tackling sexual

harassment at work, this chapter has examined sexual harassment as a form of sex discrimination and developed a moral
reason for tackling sexual harassment. The next chapter will look
at the legal reasons for employers taking a stand against sexual
harassment.

3

THE LEGAL CHALLENGE

The law is gradually being used to force a change in attitudes to sexual harassment in the workplace. Increasingly, what might have only appeared as an everyday incident at work is ending up being found to be unlawful. In law employers can be responsible for the actions of their employees. It is the responsibility of employers to ensure that their workplaces are free from sexual harassment. As public awareness grows following media interest, the number of cases will continue to increase. This trend will accelerate as women become more confident of achieving a successful outcome. With the EC Code of Practice (see Chapter 4), the pressure on employers to be aware of the issues and in particular their legal responsibilities is now even greater.

Employment law has its own particular structures and systems with cases brought to industrial tribunals and not to civil or criminal courts. Sometimes sexual harassment cases can also go to court but this is because they are taken under civil or criminal law as well as under employment law. Like any legal case, industrial tribunal cases cost money, bring the company bad publicity and sour employee relationships.

This chapter looks at the law in Britain (that is England, Wales and Scotland) as it relates to sexual harassment and describes key cases to illustrate the various legal points. Similar legislation exists in Northern Ireland. Remedies available at industrial tribunal are also described. Finally the chapter gives a brief account of how to take a case to industrial tribunal.

It is important to remember that most sexual harassment cases never go to industrial tribunal; those that do represent the tip of the iceberg. Many cases are dealt with at work, many more go totally unreported. Part of the reason is that many women are reluctant to complain, another reason is that sexual harassment can be difficult to prove as it often occurs in private.

In Britain, whether something is unlawful or not is either decided by statute – legislation passed by Parliament – or through landmark cases which have gone to the Employment Appeal Tribunal (EAT, the tribunal dealing with appeals to decisions made at industrial tribunals). This is referred to as 'judge-made law' or case law precedent.

Although the Sex Discrimination Act was introduced in 1975, it was not until 1986 that a landmark case recognized sexual harassment as potentially illegal in Britain. In that case sexual harassment was recognized as being a form of sex discrimination and therefore contravening the Sex Discrimination Act.

Since the landmark case an increasing number of cases have been brought to tribunals and an increasing number have been won. This rise in cases has accelerated over the last two years. Not all cases going to industrial tribunal are taken under the Sex Discrimination Act 1975; some are taken under the Employment Protection (Consolidation) Act 1978. It also seems likely that they could be taken under the Health and Safety Act 1974, but this has not yet been tested.

Relevant legislation in Britain

Sex Discrimination Act 1975 (SDA)

The Sex Discrimination Act covers all aspects of employment including recruitment and selection, promotion, transfers and secondment, access to training, appraisals of performance, terms and conditions of employment, access to benefits, facilities and services for employees, operation of grievance, disputes and disciplinary procedures. It also covers the provision of goods, facilities or services to the public including selling or letting of houses, business premises and land, educational establishments, clubs with more than 25 members and voluntary agencies. This means that students for example are protected by the Sex Discrimination Act.

The Sex Discrimination Act was used successfully for a sexual harassment case in 1986 (Porcelli v. Strathclyde Regional Council, discussed below). Most cases of sexual harassment are taken under this Act and nowadays more cases are won than lost. All employees are protected by the Sex Discrimination Act from the time they start work and sometimes before since the Act also covers advertising and recruiting. All employers (and bodies such as educational establishments) are liable even if they only have one employee. Under the Act sexual harassment is unlawful only if the woman's employment conditions (or educational prospects) have suffered as a result of the harassment, for example if she has lost out on promotion or training because of the harassment. In other words, sexual harassment in itself is not unlawful, whether it is unlawful or not is judged by the *effect* it has on the recipient.

The following subsections describe the relevant pieces of the Act together with the legal interpretation of sexual harassment as established through cases won at industrial tribunal.

Sexual harassment is sex discrimination
Section 1(1) holds that a person discriminates against a woman if 'on the ground of her sex he treats her less favourably than he treats or would treat a man'. As sexual harassment is by definition unwanted behaviour, a man who sexually harasses a woman is behaving in a way she does not want and she is therefore being treated less favourably than if she were a man. Sexual harassment is sex discrimination because the determining factor is the gender of the recipient. A man in a similar situation would not have been treated the same way. As Michael Rubenstein puts it:

> That not all women are sexually harassed, or that the perpetrator may single out a particular woman for harassment, does not make the behaviour any less a sex discrimination

issue. A discrimination complainant does not have to prove discrimination against the entire group to which he or she belongs; it is sufficient to show discrimination against the complainant because of her membership of the group.

(1992b: 11)

Victimization is sex discrimination

Section 4(1) holds that if a woman is victimized because she has complained this too amounts to sex discrimination since she is – through victimization – being treated less favourably than a man would be in similar circumstances. The legal argument here is that if it were not for the fact that she is a woman, she would not have been subjected to sexual harassment, she would not have had cause to complain and she would not have been victimized. If for example an employee is denied promotion, training or 'sent to Coventry' by her colleagues after making a complaint, this would count as victimization.

Quid pro quo harassment

Section 6(2)(a) holds that it is unlawful to discriminate against a woman 'in the way he affords her access to opportunities for promotion, transfer or training, or to any other benefits, facilities or services, or by refusing or deliberately omitting to afford her access to them'. Quid pro quo harassment occurs if something is given or promised in exchange for sexual favours (for example giving promotion in return for sex). Here the legality rests not on the sexual favours as such but on the outcome or threatened outcome of her rejection of his advances.

Sexual harassment puts women at a disadvantage (is a detriment)

Section 6(2)(b) holds that it is unlawful for any employer to discriminate against a woman by dismissing her or subjecting her to any detriment. A detriment means to be put at a disadvantage. A woman who is sexually harassed could be put at a disadvantage by a decision affecting her employment – for example if she does not get promotion or training opportunities because she refuses to comply with sexual advances. A woman could also be put at a disadvantage simply because she will be working in a hostile environment and therefore be at a disadvantage compared with a man working in the same environment (which for him would not be hostile), quite independently of any decision or threats being made about her employment. Similar environments can have different meanings for men and for women, for example a workplace with pornographic pictures will have a different impact on men and on women. In the same way behaviour towards a man can have a different meaning than if it is meted out towards a woman – a man putting his arm around another man's shoulders has a different meaning from a man putting his arm around a woman's shoulders. The legal test is that an environment is accepted as intimidating, hostile or humiliating if any reasonable employee would be expected to find it so. A reasonable employee does not mean the views of any reasonable person or the views of the majority of people working in that environment. For sexual harassment where the victim is a woman, it means the views of a reasonable woman. In this case it is the effect on women that is at issue whether or not the majority of people working in any one place are men. Even if other women do not object to the behaviour it does not mean that one woman cannot legitimately object, if she can show that other reasonable women could. Being put at a disadvantage also means that it is the effect of the man's behaviour that matters and not his intention. That the perpetrator did not did not intend to harass is no defence. To prove that the behaviour meted out to her was detrimental, an employee would have to give evidence such as changes in health or attendance records.

One incident can be sufficient to constitute harassment
Given that the complaint under the Sex Discrimination Act is of *detriment* – being put at a disadvantage – one act of harassment can be sufficient for a case to be taken under the Act if the incident was severe enough to cause a detriment.

Harassment of a man by a woman
Men do get harassed by women, particularly if they are in all female workplaces or in jobs that are traditionally seen as women's jobs and particularly if they are young. The Sex Discrimination Act does cover discrimination against men and so

they too could take a sexual harassment case to tribunal (they could also take a case under the Employment Protection (Consolidation) Act). There has been a legal case of harassment of a man by a woman and this was settled before reaching the tribunal. The Sex Discrimination Act also covers women or men being harassed by lesbians or gay men, since it is because of their gender that they are being harassed. But for the fact that they were a man or a woman they would not have been harassed.

Harassment of a man by a man or a woman by a woman

Harassment of lesbians or gay men by heterosexuals is not so clearly covered by the SDA since they may be harassed because of their sexuality and not because they are a woman or a man. In his manual Michael Rubenstein (1992b: 8) points out that in some sexual harassment cases of gay men by heterosexuals it could be argued that a gay man is being singled out because of his sex and could therefore have a case under the Sex Discrimination Act. The definition of sexual harassment remains the same: offensive and unwanted behaviour based on gender.

If a man is harassed because he is HIV positive, it could also be argued that this is sex discrimination because of the association of HIV/AIDS with gay men. In other words, but for the fact that he was a man he may not have been harassed because of his HIV status.

Michael Rubenstein argues that offensive remarks that are specific either to lesbians or to gay men, such as 'dyke' or 'poof', could be seen to be a 'weapon based on the sex of the victim' (1992b: 8).

The EC *Code of Practice* (see Chapter 4) specifies that harassment of lesbians and gay men is sexual harassment.

Employers are responsible for the harasser's behaviour (employer's liability)

Section 41(1) holds that employers can be liable for an employee's behaviour: 'Anything done by a person in the course of his employment shall be treated for the purposes of the Act as done by his employer as well as by him, whether or not it was done with the employer's knowledge or approval'. In most cases of sexual harassment it is the employer who is the Respondent. For the purpose of the Act 'employee' includes all those directly employed as well as those employed under contracts of service, agents of the employer or apprentices (section 81(1)). Employers are not liable for actions done outside the course of employment. As well as being liable for an employee sexually harassing another, employers can also be liable for not taking any action if they fail to deal with the woman's complaint or delay in taking action or do not keep the complainant informed of any action taken, the legal argument here being that any of these causes a detriment.

Personal liability

Under section 42(1) of the SDA anyone who aids a person to do an act unlawful under the SDA will be treated as having committed a similar unlawful act themselves. They will be treated as having aided the employer in the discriminatory act.

Joint liability

Most often, complainants name both the employer and the individual perpetrator as Respondents. In such cases compensation will be apportioned between the two.

Employers can act to avoid liability

Section 41(3) holds that an employer may be able to avoid liability even where sexual harassment has been proven or admitted if the employer took 'such steps as were reasonably practical' to prevent the harassment taking place. Such steps include things such as policy statements on sexual harassment which make clear that such behaviour is unacceptable, complaints procedures for those experiencing harassment which include the clear message that sexual harassment will not be condoned, that all complaints will be investigated and that the harasser will be disciplined if found guilty. Other steps include acting immediately when they are aware of the allegations of sexual harassment and providing sexual harassment training of all managerial staff to ensure that the policy is effectively implemented. The way an employer has handled a complaint will be taken into account in any case going to industrial tribunal.

Qualifying period
There are no qualifying periods for the Sex Discrimination Act; it protects all employees and is binding on all employers.

Time limits
Complaints must be made within three months of the date of the last incident. The last incident could be an act of victimization as a result of a complaint. In exceptional circumstances this time limit can be extended if there are very good reasons why the complainant did not bring a case at an earlier stage. Once a complaint has been lodged it can take a long time before going to industrial tribunal.

Remedies under the Sex Discrimination Act
Compensation at industrial tribunal was for up to £11,000. This figure was under dispute as it is seen to contravene European Community law and the question was referred to the European Court of Justice. The European Court of Justice has declared that it is illegal to have an upper limit in sex discrimination cases since it may mean that those who have suffered sexual discrimination may fail to recoup the financial losses they have incurred. Since November 1993 the upper limit on compensation in all sex discrimination cases has been removed. Compensation can be awarded for pecuniary loss where a person has lost income through being dismissed or having to take time off work, or where they have incurred medical costs or loss of salary through loss of promotion or other benefits. Compensation also includes damages for injury to feelings and aggravated damages if the harassment was repeated or continued over a period of time. Injury to feelings awards are the norm in sexual harassment cases. Factors that are taken into account when calculating injury to feelings include: distress to the woman, the effect on her health, her age, her vulnerability, the nature and seriousness of the harassment and long term damage to her career. Aggravated damages are rarely awarded in sexual harassment cases. To establish aggravated damages a woman must show that her sense of injury was heightened by the manner in which the defendant harassed her. For example in Veebel v. Leicester Federation of Tenants Association (described below), Mrs Veebel

was humiliated in public. On the whole sexual harassment cases have won higher compensation figures than other cases brought under the SDA. Tribunals can also require certain things of the employer, that for example the culprit be moved to another department or that the organization adopt a sexual harassment policy.

Employment Protection (Consolidation) Act 1978 (EP(C)A)

The Sex Discrimination Act, like the Race Relations Act and the Equal Pay Act, is a specialized Act affecting the relationship of employee to employer. The Employment Protection (Consolidation) Act draws together most individual rights of employees not covered by the specialized Acts. It covers various aspects of employment such as redundancy, contracts, trade union activity and employment protection. Unlike the Sex Discrimination Act it does not cover students.

Constructive dismissal

Under section 55(2)(c), an employee may find that sexual harassment at work constitutes a breach of contract and choose to resign without notice and claim *constructive dismissal*. If an employer has knowledge of harassment but does not take it seriously and fails to take reasonable steps to stop or prevent its recurrence, or allows for unreasonable procedural delays, or has an unnecessarily cumbersome appeals procedure, the employee may treat this as a breach of the implied contractual terms of mutual trust and confidence (see below, under common and civil law, for the definition of *implied contractual terms*). One aspect of the general duty of *mutual trust and confidence* is the obligation by an employer to treat grievances seriously.

Unfair dismissal

Under section 57 an employee could claim unfair dismissal if an employer terminated their employment because they refused to comply with sexual demands or complained about sexual harassment or responded to a harasser (e.g. slapped his face) or had to take time off work due to illness or stress caused by harassment.

Employees have less protection from unfair dismissal in small firms as tribunals can take into account the 'size and administrative resources of the employer's undertakings'. Options in remedies are also limited since they usually include compensation but not re-engagement.

Qualifying period
The EP(C)A only applies where the employee has been in work full time (over 16 hours a week) for two years or part time (eight to 16 hours a week) for five years, working for the same company or same employer.

Time limits
Cases of dismissal must be brought within three months of the dismissal date.

Remedies under the Employment Protection (Consolidation) Act
Employers can be ordered to reinstate, re-engage or compensate. Compensation at industrial tribunal under EP(C)A includes a basic award calculated as redundancy payment based on earnings and length of service and a compensatory award totalling a maximum of £11,000 (January 1994 figure). Cases taken under the EP(C)A can accompany a complaint under the SDA.

Health and Safety at Work Act 1974

As yet no cases have been taken under this Act. Under the Act the employer has a statutory duty to ensure the health, safety and welfare of employees at work. It may be possible for an employee to bring a case to industrial tribunal for negligence if an employer allows sexual harassment to take place given that sexual harassment is increasingly being accepted as a major health hazard.

If an employee is injured or falls ill as a result of the employer's failure to provide a safe and healthy workplace, the employee can also sue in the High Court or the county court under common law (see the section on 'other legal action' below). Among the numerous health problems that result from sexual harassment is the inability to concentrate which could have serious implications if employees become more prone to accidents. In addition to this, tension in the workplace affects the health and safety of other employees.

Additional changes following the Trade Union Reform and Employment Rights Act (TURER)

TURER was adopted by Parliament in 1993. One section concerns sexual harassment cases going to industrial tribunal. This provides for regulations to give tribunals discretionary powers to protect the parties or witnesses from being identified in reports of the proceedings. This however will not apply once the tribunal's decision has been promulgated. These new regulations should make the process of bringing an industrial tribunal complaint less distressing for the complainant and for witnesses.

Other legal action

Instead of going to industrial tribunal, it is possible in some cases of sexual harassment to use the civil or criminal courts. Industrial tribunals concentrate on the harm harassment might have done to the complainant; the courts look at the nature of the offence itself. The emphasis is therefore on the offender's behaviour and not on how it affected the person being harassed. This can be a reason for going to court as opposed to tribunal if the effect on the complainant is not clear but the harasser's behaviour is. Another advantage of going to court is that legal aid may be available for those who would normally qualify for it. In addition to this compensatory awards can be much higher than at industrial tribunal, up to £50,000 in county courts and beyond that sum in the High Court. However, the disadvantage is that the procedure is far more complex, solicitors' fees can be costly and the police may need to be involved. To date very few cases have gone to court, several have been settled out of court. Settlements can be high. The advertising agent mentioned in Chapter 1, who won a settlement of £25,000, got £18,000 more than she could have won at the time in industrial tribunal.

Civil proceedings

Civil proceedings can be instigated in the High Court or a county court in cases of sexual harassment on two grounds: first a complainant can sue the employer for *breach of contract* and second a complainant can sue the harasser for damages arising out of an *assault or intent to cause harm.*

Tribunals deal with statutory employment rights; employment contracts are subject not to statute but to common law. Common law is the unwritten law of England as it is developed through the courts. It is the law based on usage as opposed to statute. According to common law an unwritten contract exists between employee and employer. This requires that every employer provide a safe system of work, competent staff, a safe place of work and safe plant and machinery with adequate supervision.

This requirement on the employer is in addition to the employment contract agreed between employer and employee. These unwritten parts of the contract are called *implied contractual terms*. These are the terms of employment which may not be stated in a contract but which all contracts of employment include 'implicitly'. They are the terms which have been formulated over the years by the courts through case law. Under *implied contractual terms* the employer has a duty of *trust and confidence* which includes not undermining an employee's status or authority, not applying undue pressure to vary contractual terms, providing reasonable support to an employee who is victimized or harassed by workmates and a duty to protect employees from offensive sexist language. Sexual harassment cases going to court for breach of contract may be able to claim that the employer has failed in any of the above. Going to court is a course of action also open to someone who does not have a contract of employment but works for someone else on a contractual basis (for example as a consultant).

Common assault does not necessarily require physical contact but only the intention to use force or to cause physical harm. If there has been any actual or threatened physical contact, the harasser can be sued in the High Court or the county court for the *torts of assault and battery*. This covers a whole range of unwanted physical contact. Decisions are made 'on the balance of probability'. The court can also grant an injunction against the harasser.

There are no qualifying periods in civil proceedings. There is a time limit of six years from the date of dismissal for a claim of breach of contract, however.

Criminal proceedings

Criminal proceedings can be brought by the police or by an individual as a private prosecution in cases of common assault or battery, actual or grievous bodily harm, indecent assault, false imprisonment or rape. In these cases the harasser must have actually touched the complainant. Employers can support the employee against the alleged perpetrator. Cases will involve the police and can be difficult to prove as, unlike cases in the civil court, they must be shown to be 'beyond reasonable doubt'. There are no qualifying periods for criminal action.

Remedies in civil and criminal cases

Compensation is given by the Criminal Injuries Compensation Board who have the responsibility of paying compensation to victims of crime. To claim under this scheme, offences have to have been reported to the police, and victims have to co-operate but you do not have to secure a conviction.

Relevant cases

The cases listed below illustrate some of the main legal aspects of sexual harassment determined at industrial tribunal. The cases have gone to industrial tribunal under the Sex Discrimination Act and one also under the Employment Protection (Consolidation) Act.

 Sexual harassment is sex discrimination

Porcelli v. Strathclyde Regional Council (1986)
This case is considered to be the landmark for all sexual harassment cases. It was the first sexual harassment case to reach the courts (Court of Appeal and Scottish Court of Sessions)

and through it, it was established that sexual harassment is detrimental to women and therefore is a form of sex discrimination.

In 1984, Mrs Porcelli was employed by Strathclyde Council, working as a technician in a school. Two of her male colleagues ran a campaign to persuade her to leave the school. The campaign included sexual remarks and brushing up against her. She was forced to apply to transfer to another school. When she took her case to industrial tribunal under the SDA, they found that she had suffered, but they rejected the case on the grounds that a man would have suffered just as much if he had not been liked by his colleagues. But on appeal the case went to the Scottish Court of Session where it was held that the way Mrs Porcelli was treated was because she was a woman. A man would not have suffered the sexual element of his colleagues' behaviour. The court also accepted that much of the behaviour by her colleagues, even if not sexual, was aimed at her because she was a woman. This set an important precedent: that sexual harassment does not have to be *sexual* but can also include behaviour that is based on gender. By this legal point the law is in agreement with the feminist analysis of sexual harassment given in Chapter 2 that sexual harassment is about power relations between men and women. The behaviour Mrs Porcelli experienced is quite different from behaviour that results merely from a personality conflict as might have been the case if she had been a man. The court therefore concluded that Mrs Porcelli was less favourably treated than if she had been a man and that she had suffered a detriment as a result of their behaviour and that she had therefore experienced sex discrimination. The other important factor was that this established that it is the treatment not the intention that makes behaviour sexual harassment. Mrs Porcelli was awarded £3000 damages for injury to feeling.

Sexual harassment is unwanted behaviour

Johnstone v. Fenton Barns (Scotland) Ltd (1990)

Nan Johnstone was employed as a butcher in a turkey processing factory where swearing was prevalent. Mrs Johnstone did not complain about this but about other incidents involving remarks made by her colleagues which she found offensive. In one incident a colleague used a turkey neck, hanging it between his legs, saying 'how would you like that?' In another he sang a song which included the words 'put your gums on my plums, Mrs Murphy'. A third incident related to her male colleagues making sexual remarks about masturbation, a fourth incident concerned comments about menstruation. Mrs Johnstone objected to all these incidents at the time when they took place. At the tribunal the employers claimed that the incidents had to be placed in the context of the work environment, which was one where songs and jokes were commonplace. These instances could be seen as commonplace and part of acceptable behaviour in a male dominated environment, but the fact that she found them objectionable is the crucial legal point. The tribunal 'accepted that some dirty stories were told to which the applicant had not taken exception, but on the other hand we are satisfied that she had found these four particular incidents offensive and had made this clear to the participants'. The tribunal concluded that:

> If a man, working alongside a woman, converses or behaves lewdly with other people in the vicinity within earshot of the woman, and if the woman has made it clear that she finds such conduct to be offensive, then any future similar occurrences must be regarded as having taken place against her wishes, and thereby directed against her. On that view all the incidents of lewd conduct, conversation and singing which occurred after the first of them at which she complained, and which offended her, must be regarded as treatment meted out to her to which she, as a woman, was vulnerable in a way that a man would not have been, and thus as falling within the *Porcelli* concept of discrimination by means of sexual harassment.

Compensation of £3731 was awarded.

More recently in Cann v. Unilift Ltd (1992), Mrs Cann lost her case because she had not made it clear to the harasser that his behaviour was unwelcome.

Victimization following a complaint under the SDA is illegal

Veebel v. Leicester Federation of Tenants Associations (1989)

Pia Veebel was given a period of training before she started her job with the Federation of Tenants Associations. During her training the chairman, Mr Lindsey, made several sexual remarks to her and put his arms around her. After she began the job itself this behaviour continued. He would repeatedly put his arm around her, press her against him or kiss her. She told him she did not want him to behave in this way. Finally, she handed in her resignation. Mr Lindsey begged her to reconsider, so she stayed on. After this, there were no more incidents but Mr Lindsey's attitude changed. Pia Veebel was 'publicly humiliated' at a conference among other vindictive incidents. Ms Veebel resigned. The industrial tribunal upheld her complaint finding that she had been discriminated against and had suffered a detriment by being subjected to an 'intolerable working environment'. They also held that this was aggravated by the manner in which Mr Lindsey behaved. She was awarded £2250 for injury to feeling and aggravated damages.

One incident is enough to count as sexual harassment

Heads v. (1) Insitu Cleaning Co. Ltd and (2) Brown (1992)

A single remark to an area supervisor by her manager was sufficient to amount to sex discrimination. Mrs Heads was in a meeting when her manager, Mr Brown, came in and greeted her by saying 'Hiya, big tits'. The tribunal concluded 'the single remark made by Mr Brown was sufficiently serious to constitute a detriment and therefore discrimination'.

Harassment of a woman by a woman

There has been at least one case where a lesbian harassment victim won her case (Johnson and Garbutt v. Gateway Foodmarkets Ltd, 1990). Miss Garbutt and Miss Johnson were employed in the Red Balloon Restaurant. Their supervisor was Una Cooper. Miss Johnson complained to management that Mrs Cooper had put her hand at the top of her thigh. The incident was witnessed by other staff. Mrs Cooper was suspended on full pay pending an inquiry. During the inquiry Miss Garbutt revealed that she also had been touched on some occasions by Mrs Cooper. She said that Mrs Cooper had on several occasions squeezed her bottom. It was not as if she was patting her: 'it was more like the touching of a boyfriend'. However, the employers believed Mrs Cooper when she said that it was all meant to be a joke. They gave her a final warning but let her return to work. Miss Johnson and Miss Garbutt refused to work with her. They were dismissed on the grounds of gross misconduct for refusing to obey. The tribunal found that at no stage had Mrs Cooper ever sexually harassed any man and that she would not have done so. They concluded that Mrs Cooper would not have treated Miss Johnson or Miss Garbutt in the same way had they been men. The tribunal also found that the employers had unlawfully victimized Miss Johnson and Miss Garbutt.

Miss Garbutt was awarded £2361 for unfair dismissal (under the EP[C]A) and £750 under the SDA. Miss Johnson was awarded £1000 damages for injury to feeling under the SDA (she did not qualify for a claim under the EP(C)A).

Harassment of a man by a man

Gates v. Security Express Guards (1993) was about a young man experiencing harassment from his male supervisor. On many occasions the supervisor, Mr Bradbury, had made sexual remarks to Mr Gates and simulated sex in front of him with another security officer. Mr Gates requested a transfer from days to nights so as to avoid being in contact with Mr Bradbury. However, soon after the transfer Mr Bradbury came up behind him and 'put one hand around his waist and one hand around his neck and then attempted to simulate anal sexual intercourse with him'. The tribunal found that the supervisor's conduct was 'unwanted, unreasonable and offensive to the applicant'. Mr Gates was awarded £4500 including £1500 for injury to feelings.

Employer liability

Enterprise Glass Co. Ltd v. Miles (1990)
Soon after she joined Enterprise Glass Co. Ltd, Ms Miles was harassed by another employee, Mr Peake. He repeatedly made

remarks of a suggestive or sexual nature which Ms Miles found offensive. She complained to one of the managers, Mr Cooper, who told her not to worry. As the harassment continued she made a formal complaint. Mr Cooper said he needed positive evidence that the harassment was occurring, so Ms Miles taped a conversation with Mr Peake. In response Mr Cooper moved Ms Miles to another department. Two weeks later she was back to her old department and Mr Peake was told by Mr Cooper to stop or he would be given a formal written warning which could eventually lead to dismissal. Soon after Mr Peake was promoted to supervisor and the harassment began again. Ms Miles complained to Mr Cooper again, but he said he was too busy and she should ignore Mr Peake's comments. Eventually Ms Miles left and took a case against the employer and against Mr Peake himself. The industrial tribunal ruled that Ms Miles had suffered sexual harassment and that the behaviour constituted a breach of the SDA. Furthermore the company had failed to show that it had taken reasonable steps to prevent the harassment occurring since Mr Cooper did not follow up his earlier warning with action against Mr Peake. Merely warning employees about sexual harassment without taking further disciplinary action when sexual harassment continues is not sufficient to absolve an employer from liability for employees' conduct under the Sex Discrimination Act. Mr Peake was ordered to pay Ms Miles £750 in compensation, and the company to pay her £1000.

Taking prompt and appropriate action may however not be enough. In another case, Carter v. Westcliff Hall Sidmouth Ltd (1990), the tribunal held that:

> it is not enough simply to take action as soon as an act occurs: something must be done to prevent it occurring in the first place, if there were any reasonable steps that could have been taken . . . there was no reference to sexual harassment in the employer's staff handbook.

Sexual harassment can be a breach of contract and result in constructive dismissal

Bracebridge Engineering Ltd v. Darby (1990)
One day before leaving work, Mrs Darby was grabbed by two members of staff senior to herself, and forced into an office where

she was held upside down while they made sexual comments about her and touched her private parts. She managed to get away and complained the next morning to the general manager. However both men involved denied the incident ever took place and nothing more was done. Mrs Darby resigned and took her case to industrial tribunal where she won her case under the Sex Discrimination Act for sexual harassment and under the Employment Protection (Consolidation) Act for constructive dismissal. The employers appealed claiming that one incident cannot count as sexual harassment, that the staff concerned were not acting in the course of their employment and that the detriment suffered by Mrs Darby was not in the context of her employment. The Appeal Court ruled that one incident of sexual harassment does fall within the meaning of the Act if it is sufficiently serious as to discriminate against a woman because she is a woman; that she had suffered a detriment in her employment since the staff involved were her charge-hand and works manager; that the staff involved were acting in the course of their employment since they were both engaged in disciplinary and supervisory functions; finally that Mrs Darby was entitled to claim that she had been constructively dismissed because her complaint was not seriously investigated by management. The Appeal Court also ruled that the tribunal was right to find that the term relating to the mutual obligation of trust, confidence and support and the obligation not to undermine the confidence of the female staff had been breached. Compensation of £3050 was awarded.

Taking a case to industrial tribunal

This section gives advice for trade unions or voluntary organizations or anyone else taking a case to industrial tribunal. Preparing a case for industrial tribunal and representing someone at industrial tribunal are both complicated and for those without experience should be done with the help of specialist agencies. This section merely gives some basic advice on helping complainants prepare for industrial tribunal. More detailed guides are available from the Equal Opportunities Commission (EOC) or from Women Against Sexual Harassment (WASH). Addresses are given in Appendix 6.

Before thinking of going to an industrial tribunal employees (or students) should be advised to use the grievance procedure so long as there is not a risk of running out of time since complaints to industrial tribunal need to be made within three months. The use of a complaints or grievance procedure is covered in Chapter 5. Any employee who has worked for at least 13 weeks is entitled by law to a written statement of their terms and conditions which should include who to go to if they have a grievance. Employees have a right to ask to see the grievance procedure. There are no such rights for students even though they are covered by the Sex Discrimination Act.

If an employee decides that they want to go to industrial tribunal they should be advised that they need support. It can be a lengthy business, and proving a case can be difficult. Not all cases succeed. Support would most usually be given by a trade union. If this is not practical then help is available from Law Centres, the EOC, some Citizen's Advice Bureaux (CABs), WASH and other voluntary organizations such as the City Centre Project (addresses are in Appendix 6). It is also possible to contact individual solicitors who deal in employment law, but this is expensive. Legal aid is not available for representation at industrial tribunals but is available for advice and assistance. Legal advice is free from Law Centres, CABs or ACAS (Advisory, Conciliation and Arbitration Service). Trade unions will give free legal assistance to their members and the EOC may give financial assistance for cases taken under the SDA. Solicitors may give the first half hour of their advice for a cheap standard fee.

Any complaints to industrial tribunals must be with the Central Office of Industrial Tribunals (COIT – address in Appendix 6) no later than three months after the alleged harassment took place or three months after a woman has left her employment if she was forced to leave because of the harassment. If it is later than that it may still be possible to put in a complaint if there are very good reasons for the lateness. If a complaint cannot be taken to an industrial tribunal because the time limit has passed it may be possible to go to court for personal injury or breach of contract (time limits of three years and six years respectively), but this will depend on the case.

If someone comes for advice and does want to pursue legal

action, two forms need to be filled in. One will need to be sent to COIT and the other (a questionnaire) to the Respondent (the person against whom the complaint is made – employer or harasser). It is wise to name both as Respondents. Cases can be taken under several Acts at the same time, the SDA and the EP(C)A for example. If this course of action is followed it should be clearly indicated on the form. Forms can be obtained from an Employment Office, a CAB, a Law Centre or from COIT itself. Any adviser should also make a summary of the case, noting where the person worked, what they did, how long they had worked for, whether they belong to a trade union, why and when they left (if they did). Advisers should also write down a brief outline of events, noting the name of the harasser, his job, the dates of the harassment, details of what happened and what action was taken by the complainant or by anyone else.

In 1994 cases were taking approximately a year to reach a hearing at industrial tribunal (IT). A complainant can withdraw their case at any time right up to the time of the case being heard at IT. Advisers should inform complainants of this; nothing is lost by putting in a case to IT as they can always change their minds later.

Claims to industrial tribunals are often settled out of court. Any such agreement should be put in an official document by ACAS.

Conclusion

Although sexual harassment is not in the statute books it is potentially unlawful. Most cases are taken under the Sex Discrimination Act. Most often the employer is named as the Respondent, although increasingly it is both the employer and the alleged harasser. Apart from being degrading and undermining for the woman, any case is bad publicity for employers and often leads to a lowering of morale in the workforce. Developing a sexual harassment policy can help avoid legal challenge; it can help prevent sexual harassment at work; it helps in dealing with any sexual harassment that does occur at work and in the event of a case going to industrial tribunal a sexual harassment policy will go some way towards protecting the employer. It gives out a clear message to employees that sexual harassment is taken seriously. This will go a long way to establishing a culture whereby employees, both male and female, can work in a safe open environment where each individual is valued for their own work. How this is done will be the topic of Chapter 5.

The most recent cases of sexual harassment take account not only of British law but also of European law and notably the Code of Practice on sexual harassment. The code came out of an EC Resolution on sexual harassment which represented, in many ways, an important new development to the way in which we approach issues of sexual harassment. This is explained in the next chapter.

4

PROTECTING THE DIGNITY OF WOMEN AND MEN AT WORK: THE EC CODE OF PRACTICE

Sexual harassment in Europe is widespread. Around four million people within the European Union (EU) have experienced sexual harassment (Collins 1992). In Belgium, surveys showed that 30 to 34 per cent of women are sexually harassed at work; in Spain the figure is around 80 per cent rising to 90 per cent among young women; in Portugal the figure is 37 per cent, in Holland 58 per cent and in Germany 72 per cent (Rubenstein 1992b: 7). Survey after survey shows that sexual harassment is damaging to the women who experience it, to those who witness it and to employers through absenteeism and reduced profitability.

Since early in its inception there has been European Community legislation that could be used to protect women against harassment but nothing was specific. The issue had not been addressed in a unifying way and by the early 1980s there was pressure to address what was seen by women's groups as a very serious problem. In 1991, the European Commission issued a Code of Practice on sexual harassment.

The Code took five years to produce. Its roots lay in a request from the European Council in 1986 for the Commission to study sexual harassment. The results of this initial study were published in 1988, and after intense lobbying by women's organizations in May 1990 the European Community published its 'Resolution on the protection of the dignity of women and men at work'. This resolution, which was a statement of intent, was then followed in November 1991 by a 'Recommendation on the protection of the dignity of women and men at work', a Code of Practice on sexual harassment and a declaration on the implementation of the Recommendation and the Code of Practice.

This chapter first describes European Union legislation (the European Community, EC, became the European Union, EU, in November 1993) and its application to the UK. It will then look specifically at the main elements of the Recommendation and the Code of Practice on sexual harassment and how these have been implemented in the various member states. It will also look at some recent UK cases where the Code of Practice has been used in tribunal decisions.

EU legislation: How it is made and how it affects the UK

The EU legislative process is complicated. Initially new legislation is proposed by the European Commission (the EU civil service) which consults the European Parliament, but it is the Council of Ministers that votes on new legislation. The Council of Ministers, which is the main decision making body in the EU, is made up of representative ministers from each member state. The European Court of Justice is responsible for interpreting EU law. This court is made up of judges from each member state. Its decisions override national legislation and are binding on member states.

Legal instruments in the EU

There are several ways by which the EU sets down the legal framework in which member states work.

- *Treaties* such as the Treaty of Rome and the Maastricht Treaty must be considered as legal instruments because they contain articles that have legislative force in themselves.

- *Directives* lay down *objectives* to be met by member states within a stated period of time. In the UK this usually means that bills are passed and acts made or amended (in Parliament legislation is passed as a 'bill' which is then turned into an 'act' when it becomes law). In each member state the result of the objectives must be legally binding but it is up to the state to work out its own method for meeting the objectives. A *directive* is directly enforceable against any state or against the state in its capacity as an employer. This means that if, for example, the UK does not comply with a directive by not passing appropriate national legislation it can be taken to the European Court of Justice by the EU. If it does not comply with the directive in relation to the people the state employs, that is to say if it is not applying the directive directly to those it employs without necessarily adopting national legislation, it is again in breach of the directive. In the UK, for example, the Equal Treatment Directive would be applicable within the civil service where employees could appeal directly to the Directive at industrial tribunal or in the courts without the need to invoke UK law. All other employees wishing to appeal to the Directive can only bring cases under UK law. Directives therefore have to be translated into national legislation (unless national laws already cover the relevant points). The Equal Treatment Directive is covered in this country by the Sex Discrimination Act 1975 which in fact predated it (see the first section of Chapter 3).
- *Codes of practice* (such as the one on sexual harassment) are not legislative measures themselves, however in 1993 the Code of Practice on Sexual Harassment was being used in tribunals (see the section on the use of the EC Code of Practice in the UK, below).
- *Resolutions and recommendations* have no direct force in law but do have to be taken into account by courts and tribunals when reaching decisions even though the state's own legislation provides the main framework. For example, the European Court of Justice ruled in a Belgian case, Grimaldi v. Fonds des Maladies Professionnelles (1989), that 'domestic courts are bound to take Recommendations into consideration in order to decide disputes submitted to them, in particular where they are capable of clarifying the interpretation of other provisions of national or Community law'.

The EU legal process

To appeal to European law an individual must first go through the national courts or tribunals. If satisfaction is not reached in local courts and tribunals individuals can, in the last resort, appeal to the European Court of Justice (ECJ). This is the final court of appeal. As yet no sexual harassment cases in the UK have gone to the ECJ. Before the UK joined the EU the House of Lords was the final court of appeal. However, EU law can only be appealed to if local courts fail and if the case raises a question of community law.

For example, the case of Mrs Marshall (a sex discrimination case) was taken to the ECJ; Mrs Marshall had won a discrimination case at industrial tribunal in 1980 when she complained that her employers retired her at 62 when men were allowed to retire at 65. The industrial tribunal awarded her £6250 compensation which was the maximum allowed in UK law at the time although her loss of earnings (resulting from early retirement) amounted to £19,000. Following a 13 year legal battle, the ECJ have ruled that the limit set by industrial tribunals is illegal as it is not in the spirit of the Equal Treatment Directive since it means that women cannot get true redress through the legal system.

If a case is taken to the European Court, it is returned to local courts for enforcement once the European Court has made a decision. Remedies are left to national courts to decide. In the Marshall case mentioned above, the ruling on the illegality of limits for compensation also means that the UK government will have to amend British legislation to take this into account. If a decision is made in any member state on the basis of European law it can have implications for all EU states. Court rulings by the ECJ on a case in Belgium, for example, have implications for residents in the UK. Such a decision can be appealed to directly in local courts or tribunals.

Sexual harassment and European Union law

The EU refers to the Equal Treatment Directive (passed in 1976) as the relevant legislative instrument on sexual harassment. The Directive outlaws sex discrimination in training, promotion, working conditions and dismissal. It also outlaws any reference to marital or family status in any of these areas.

The Recommendation on sexual harassment is not in itself a legal instrument, it refers to the Equal Treatment Directive as the proper legal remedy. In many countries the fact that sexual harassment is a form of sex discrimination and therefore comes under the Equal Treatment Directive has not been tested. It has in the UK since the Porcelli case in 1986 (see Chapter 3) where sexual harassment cases are usually taken under the Sex Discrimination Act. The new Recommendation on sexual harassment should make this process easier for other EU states, and legitimize what already happens in the UK.

The EC 1991 Recommendation on sexual harassment

The Recommendation followed a Resolution which came out of the Commission's report on *The Dignity of Women and Men at Work* produced in 1988. The report argued that sexual harassment is

> conduct at the workplace which is a proven risk to health and safety, which imposes substantial costs upon employers, which fundamentally conflicts with the principle of equal treatment of men and women and undermines its objective, and yet for which there is no appropriate legal remedy available. The case for a Community initiative is overwhelming.
>
> (Rubenstein 1992b: 50)

The report called for a directive on sexual harassment. The EC decided not to issue a directive which would have had more legal force but instead issued a resolution, then a recommendation.

The Resolution on sexual harassment

The Resolution is fairly short; it affirms that 'conduct of a sexual nature, or other conduct based on sex affecting the dignity of women and men at work, including conduct of superiors and colleagues, constitutes an intolerable violation of the dignity of workers or trainees and is unacceptable'. The Resolution calls on member states to remind employers that they have a responsibility to seek to ensure that the work environment is free from sexual harassment. It also calls for member states to develop campaigns and promote awareness. The Resolution calls on the Commission to 'continue its efforts to inform and make aware employers, workers . . . lawyers and members of courts . . . that failure to accept the definition given of sexual harassment may be contrary to the principle of equal treatment'. The Resolution further asks the Commission to draw up,

> in consultation with the social partners and following consultation with the Member States and national equal opportunities authorities, a Code of Practice on the protection of the dignity of women and men at work which will provide guidance based on examples and best practice in the Member States.

The Recommendation on sexual harassment

The Recommendation aims to promote awareness that sexual harassment is sex discrimination and contrary to the principle of equal treatment, to provide a basis for definition of sexual harassment and to encourage the practical application of positive measures to deal with the problem – both preventative and procedural. Article 1 of the Recommendation says:

> It is recommended that the Member States take action to promote awareness that conduct of a sexual nature, or other conduct based on sex affecting the dignity of women and men at work, including conduct of superiors and colleagues, is unacceptable if:
>
> (a) such conduct is unwanted, unreasonable and offensive to the recipient;
> (b) a person's rejection of, or submission to, such conduct on the part of employers or workers is used explicitly or implicitly as a basis for a decision which affects that person's access to vocational training, access to employment, continued employment, promotion, salary or any other employment decisions;

(c) such conduct creates an intimidating, hostile or humiliating work environment for the recipient.

Article 2 of the Recommendation asks that member states take action to implement the Code of Practice in the public sector and Article 3 states that member states should encourage the private sector to implement the Code.

The legal status of resolutions and recommendations

As mentioned above, the Recommendation does, in referring to sexual harassment, state 'that such conduct may, in certain circumstances, be contrary to the principle of equal treatment within the meaning of Articles 3, 4 and 5 of Directive 76/207/EEC' (the Equal Treatment Directive). In the first section of this chapter, we saw that resolutions and recommendations do not have the legal force of directives and are on the whole considered as representing the political will of the EU and as having simply moral value. They do however need to be taken into account by the courts and tribunals and to this extent have some legal power. This new type of Community law has been called 'soft law'. In this case the Recommendation makes it clear that it is meant to help interpretation of the Equal Treatment Directive in those cases of discrimination which take the form of sexual harassment.

The 1991 Code of Practice

The Code of Practice is the practical application of the Recommendation. It aims to provide steps to create an environment where sexual harassment does not occur; it is intended to be relevant to both the public and private sectors. Small and medium-sized organizations are advised to adapt some of the recommendations and possibly cooperate with other organizations in the same industry or locality. In 1993 the European Commission published a guide to implementing the Code of Practice, *How to Combat Sexual Harassment at Work*. The guide is aimed at employers and trade unions. In the foreword it warns employers that:

> Turning a blind eye to sexual harassment costs time and money. Organizations should think seriously about the cumulative cost of replacing staff affected, paying sick leave to employees who miss work because of stress, and the implications of reduced individual and group productivity – all expensive drains on the morale and efficiency of workplace teams.
>
> (European Commission 1993: 6)

The following is a summary of the Code.

Definition of sexual harassment

The Code gives a definition of sexual harassment along the same lines as that given in the Resolution and Recommendation quoted above. It also gives examples from the range of behaviour that could count as harassment, adding that sexual harassment is nothing to do with romance, that 'the essential characteristic of sexual harassment is that it is *unwanted* by the recipient, that it is for each individual to determine what behaviour is acceptable to them and what they regard as offensive'. The guide then adds that the right to be treated with dignity is an individual right; 'in particular it is not dependent upon the culture of the workplace or subject to the majority view of colleagues. That others acquiesce in a working environment polluted by sexual harassment does not deprive an individual of her or his right to object' (1993: 25). The guide reaffirms that sexual harassment is sex discrimination adding that

> the fact that a perpetrator may single out a particular woman for sexual harassment does not make the behaviour any less a sex discrimination issue. It is a fundamental principle of equal treatment law that a complainant does not have to prove discrimination against the whole group to which they belong: it is sufficient to show discrimination

against the complainant because of her membership of the group. (1993: 32)

The Code specifically includes in this definition harassment of men by women and harassment on the grounds of sexuality (being a lesbian or a gay man). The guide also makes a link with harassment on the grounds of race (1993: 15), pointing out that sexual harassment is often combined with racial harassment, that, for example, with black women racist language will often form a large part of the harassment.

The law and employer's responsibilities

Michael Rubenstein holds that since the Recommendation and the Code of Practice supplement each other, industrial tribunals are bound to take into account their content and that 'in particular, a Tribunal is likely to find that an employer who has not followed the recommendations set out in the Code has not taken reasonably practical steps to prevent sexual harassment so as to escape liability under s.41(3)' (of the SDA, see Chapter 3) (1992b: 20).

The Code itself points out that sexual harassment may be contrary to the Equal Treatment Directive as it is a form of sex discrimination. The Code adds that 'As sexual harassment is often a function of women's status in the employment hierarchy, policies to deal with sexual harassment will be most effective where they are linked to a broader policy to promote equal opportunities and to improve the position of women'. According to the Code sexual harassment may also be seen as a risk to health and safety. On managers' responsibilities the guide to the Code states that the attitude and conduct of managers must serve as an example to all their staff, in addition to this 'managers should keep their eyes and ears open for the various forms of sexual harassment and intervene if they observe them' (1993: 51).

Trade unions

The Code also covers collective bargaining, recommending joint working between employers and trade unions on policies. Recommendations to trade unions include 'that trade unions should formulate and issue clear policy statements on sexual harassment and take steps to raise awareness of the problem of sexual harassment in the workplace, in order to help create a climate in which it is neither condoned nor ignored'. Trade unions also have a role to negotiate policies with employers (see the first section of Chapter 6 for more details).

Sexual harassment policies

For the prevention of sexual harassment the Code recommends adopting a policy 'which expressly states that all employees have a right to be treated with dignity [and] that sexual harassment at work will not be permitted or condoned'. The duty of managers and employees to abide by the policy should be specified. The guide to the Code adds that

a policy statement goes further than a general statement of the employer's intent to do something. In a policy statement, the employer should address the employees directly and specify exactly what they can expect from the management and what the management expects from employees. The object of the statement should be to convince everyone that there is no place for sexual harassment in the organization.

(1993: 46)

Procedures for dealing with cases of sexual harassment should be made clear. Policies should state that the issue will be dealt with seriously, expediently and confidentially; and that employees will be protected against victimization. A policy should also specify the disciplinary measures which will be taken if an employee is found guilty.

The Code then goes through issues such as communicating the policy, training managers and training those who will be responsible for any official role in the complaints procedure.

Sexual harassment complaints

On the procedures to be adopted, the Code recommends having procedures which allow for complaints to be resolved informally in the first instance. The Code goes on to advise 'that employers should designate someone to provide advice and assistance to employees subjected to sexual harassment, where possible, with responsibilities to assist in the resolution of any problems, whether through informal or normal means'. On the complaints procedure itself, the Code recommends that

> a formal procedure should specify to whom the employee should bring a complaint, and it should also provide an alternative if in the particular circumstances the normal grievance procedure may not be suitable, for example because the accused harasser is the employee's line manager. It is also advisable to make provision for employees to bring a complaint in the first instance to someone of their own sex.

The Code adds that employers should monitor and review the procedures.

On the investigation process, the Code recommends dealing with all complaints sensitively, adding that 'those carrying out the investigation should not be connected with the allegation in any way'. Both the complainant and the alleged harasser should have the right to be accompanied by a trade union representative or a friend. Records should be kept of all meetings.

On disciplinary offences 'it is recommended that violations of the organisation's policy . . . should be treated as a disciplinary offence'. If a complaint is upheld and someone needs to be relocated, the complainant should be given the choice to remain in her job if she wishes.

In conclusion the Code stresses the responsibility of employees stating that they

> have a clear role to play in helping to create a climate at work in which sexual harassment is unacceptable. They can contribute to preventing sexual harassment through an awareness and sensitivity towards the issue and by ensuring that standards of conduct for themselves and for colleagues do not cause offence.

Declaration on sexual harassment

The final statement to come from the EC on sexual harassment was a Declaration, issued in November 1991 (see Rubenstein

1992b). It came from the Council of European Communities (the highest body in the EU) and said that the Council:

1 endorses the general objective of the Commission Recommendation;
2 invites the member states to develop and implement coherent, integrated policies to prevent and combat sexual harassment at work;
3 asks that within three years of the Declaration a report be drawn up by the Commission looking at the effectiveness of the Code of Practice. To date (October 1994), this has not been done. However, a report on 'Confidential Counsellors' was published in 1994.

Policies and legal remedies across the EU

Independently from the Recommendation the following legislation could be used in sexual harassment cases in the EU: in all member states sexual harassment would be treated as a criminal offence where there has been actual physical assault or molestation. In addition to this, in most countries employers have a duty not to undermine the employee's dignity or integrity as a worker. In the UK this is the employer's duty of 'mutual trust and confidence'. In other countries this is referred to variously as 'obligations relating to physical, emotional and psychological working conditions'; 'a duty to maintain physical and moral integrity'; 'offences against the personality' or 'respect for the dignity of workers'.

Following the Recommendation, all EU states have now had cases on sexual harassment which have established that dismissal for refusing to submit to sexual advances or victimization for complaining about harassment is unlawful. The following subsections outline some of the measures member states have taken specifically as a result of the Recommendation.

France

New legislation has been introduced on sexual harassment, 'Abuse of authority at the workplace in sexual matters' (1991).

The new law amends both the Labour Code and the Penal Code to include sexual harassment. The definition given for sexual harassment is very narrow: 'a word, gesture, attitude or behaviour by a hierarchical superior with a view to compelling a employee to respond to a solicitation of a sexual nature'. This is what is termed 'quid pro quo harassment' – asking for sexual favours in exchange for getting a job, promotion etc. Firing an employee who refuses sexual favours is illegal. Employers are asked to introduce measures to combat sexual harassment at work and to discipline managers who harass their employees. The French law ignores harassment between colleagues. Fines can be for up to, approximately, the equivalent of £10,500; imprisonment can be up to one year.

Belgium

A Royal Decree to protect workers against sexual harassment at work came into effect in 1992. According to the Decree employers shall be obliged to state in their work regulations the measures they have to protect employees against sexual harassment:

> these measures shall especially encompass a policy statement concerning sexual harassment at work, the designation of a confidential counsellor . . . the complaints-handling procedures and the disciplinary measures that may be taken. Sexual harassment includes any form of verbal or physical conduct of a sexual nature which the perpetrator knows, or should know, infringes upon the dignity of women and men at work.
>
> (Article 1 of the Decree)

Italy

Unions have set up support groups staffed by women and telephone help lines. Sexual harassment is taken to courts under health and safety legislation.

Spain

A worker's charter was issued in 1989 stating that 'respect for a person's privacy and dignity, including protection against verbal or physical insults of a sexual nature' must be ensured by all employers. This has no legal standing but represents an 'agreement' between employers and their employees. Most workplaces now have agreements that recognize that sexual harassment can be either from a manager or from a colleague. The penalty is from one month's suspension from work for harassment of a colleague to three months suspension for harassment of a junior.

Denmark

A national collective agreement between employers and employees has been reached. This requires employers to adopt policies on sexual harassment but has no legal force.

The Netherlands

The government has included sexual harassment in health and safety legislation.

Germany

A Regional Anti-Discrimination Act in the State of Berlin was passed in 1991. Section 12 of the Act states that: 'The responsibilities of employees in managerial positions include combating the sexual harassment of employees and investigating cases when they become known', 'sexual harassment is a breach of the employee's duty', and 'a recipient must not suffer disadvantages as a result of submitting a complaint'.

Ireland

Sexual harassment is seen as coming under the Employment Equality Act of 1977. Recently employers have produced guidelines on sexual harassment.

Britain

In 1992 the government issued a leaflet, *Sexual Harassment in the Workplace*, produced by the Employment Department and sent it to all employers with more than 10 staff, advising them on their responsibilities with regard to sexual harassment. The leaflet draws attention to the fact that sexual harassment may contravene the Sex Discrimination Act.

Cases in the UK where the EC Code of Practice has been used

In the last 18 months, the EC Code has been used with increasing frequency in UK tribunal cases. So far all these cases have referred to the Code to clarify the definition of sexual harassment. The Code could, no doubt, be used to clarify other things such as the duty put on employers to provide a sexual harassment policy as well as a complaints procedure relevant to sexual harassment cases. It will be interesting to see what further use British tribunals make of the Code.

In Wadman v. Carpenter Farrer Partnership (1993), the Employment Appeals Tribunal (EAT) recommends that the definition of sexual harassment given in the Code of Practice 'may be of some assistance to tribunals in considering these matters' (*Equal Opportunities Review Case Law Digest* 1993b: 3). The definition was used by the EAT in this case.

Tofield v. Pollicino t/a Donnabella Hair Design (1992) was another case at industrial tribunal which used the Code. Tracey Tofield was a hairdresser trainee. She resigned after a series of sexual incidents which culminated in her male boss asking her if she would encircle the thumb of one hand with a ring made by the thumb and index finger of the other, and move them up and down so as to simulate masturbation. The Newcastle-upon-Tyne tribunal noted that the EC Code of Practice defines sexual harassment as 'unwanted conduct of a sexual nature or other conduct based on sex affecting the dignity of women and men at work'. Tracey Tofield was found to have been discriminated against by conduct which amounted to sexual harassment.

Donnelly v. Watson Grange Ltd (1992) is another case where the Code's definition was used. Elaine Donnelly was dismissed from her job as a sales executive. She brought a case to industrial tribunal complaining that the marketing manager included sexual connotations in everything he said to her. The tribunal however dismissed the complaint saying: 'there can be no doubt that to describe a lady as a bit of a crumpet, or to refer to her as being a big girl, or to suggest that she should get between the sheets with a buyer in order to get business, can amount to sexual harassment'. The problem was that Elaine Donnelly had not made it clear that this was *unwanted behaviour* and therefore it cannot be seen to be sexual harassment. In its decision the tribunal referred to the Code of Practice saying that

> the essential characteristic of sexual harassment is that it is unwanted by the recipient and that it is for each individual to determine what behaviour is acceptable to them and what they regard as offensive. In the view of the tribunal, remarks of the type which have been listed could reasonably be totally unacceptable to a female employee, and if she made the fact that it was unacceptable clear and it was persisted in then it would be sexual harassment.
> (quoted in *Equal Opportunities Review Case Law Digest* 1993a: 4)

In another case, Gates v. Security Express Guards (1993) (described in more detail in Chapter 3), an industrial tribunal referred to the Code of Practice and stated that:

> it is quite clear that the conduct of Mr Bradbury was both unwanted, unreasonable and offensive to the applicant. Furthermore, it is also quite clear that the conduct was intimidating and humiliating and unwanted insofar as the working environment was concerned.
> (quoted in *Equal Opportunities Review Case Law Digest* 1993c: 3)

Conclusion

This chapter has looked at the EU's approach to sexual harassment. The Code of Practice and the Guide to Implementing the Code do much more than articulate legal requirements. They both formulate policies which should be followed by employers and trade unions. These policies, and their accompanying recommendations, are similar to, and complemented by, the guidance and proposals given in the next chapter.

5

DEVELOPING SEXUAL HARASSMENT POLICIES

Chapter 3 showed that there are legal obligations on employers to have a sexual harassment policy. Chapter 4 outlined the European Union's initiatives on sexual harassment which strengthen the legal obligations. But quite apart from the law, as we saw in Chapter 1, a sexual harassment policy, by improving the working conditions of a large proportion of the workforce (women), is good for business. This chapter looks at sexual harassment policies. It goes through the steps that should be taken to ensure that a successful policy is in place and is fully operational. All that is said in this chapter about managers would equally apply in an educational establishment to teachers or academic staff.

The chapter looks at:

1 Developing a sexual harassment policy:
   - why have a sexual harassment policy?
   - allocating responsibility;
   - consultation with trade unions or staff associations;
   - writing a policy statement.

2 Areas to be covered by a sexual harassment policy:
   - definition of sexual harassment;
   - complaints procedures;
   - malicious complaints;

- appeals;
- disciplinary procedures;
- the role of advisers.

3 Implementing a sexual harassment policy:
- managers' responsibility;
- training staff and advisers;
- communicating the policy to all staff;
- changing the culture;
- setting up monitoring, evaluation and review procedures.

Before drafting a sexual harassment policy organizations should introduce an equal opportunities policy. Some organizations have sexual harassment as part of their equal opportunities policy. It is much better to have them separate for two reasons. First, the issues each policy needs to address are different – an equal opportunities policy aims to redress discrimination against women in general and this might go some way towards changing the context in which sexual harassment can occur (see Chapter 2). Whereas an equal opportunities policy concentrates largely on policy changes, a sexual harassment policy deals with more personal issues and is specifically about the impact of one person's behaviour on another person. Second, combining the two would make a very heavy and unwieldy document which in practice would be more difficult to implement.

In drawing up a policy a company will shape the culture of the organization by establishing a set of standards for behaviour within the workplace. Any policy should make it clear that the company will not tolerate sexual harassment and that all staff, regardless of gender, have the right to be treated with dignity and respect. Some organizations choose to issue one policy covering all forms of harassment (racial, sexual, harassment of disabled people, lesbians and gay men and so on). The same principles would apply in this case as for a policy which covers only sexual harassment. Any harassment policy should be drawn up in consultation with trade unions. No company is too small to have a policy. Policies should be relevant to the particular organization, they should not be simply copied from another company. Research done by WASH (1992) shows that employers who find it difficult introducing sexual harassment policies and relating them to specific organizational needs have little success in tackling sexual harassment at work. Ideally a policy should cover all relevant constituents of an organization's sphere of work: paid staff working within the organization itself, contracted staff, clients, directors, volunteers and members of committees (this would include management committee members in voluntary organizations, advisory committee members, boards of directors, governors) and elected members (for local authorities and central government).

The first and most crucial step in developing a policy is to decide to adopt one. The most senior people in the organization should take and embrace this decision. The decision should include who will be drawing up the policy and whether outside advice will need to be sought. A timescale for drawing up the policy should be set.

Developing a sexual harassment policy

Why have a sexual harassment policy?

Organizations which do not have sexual harassment policies often claim that there is no need for such a policy since there is no evidence within the company of instances of harassment; there have been no complaints. However, as we saw in Chapter 1, this does not mean that sexual harassment does not occur in the organization. Women may not complain because they don't know that they can complain, or how to complain and what will happen if they do. Women who experience sexual harassment often suffer in silence; they are embarrassed, don't want to be seen as a troublemaker, fear victimization and want to keep their job. They fear that they will not be taken seriously if they complain, frequently they do not want the harasser to get into trouble – they just want him to stop. Most women do not dare complain unless they feel that it is safe to do so. Women who are being harassed lose their self-confidence, become demotivated, feel undervalued, suffer stress and make more mistakes at work. The resulting action is that women just leave their jobs, a cost loss to the company and a loss to the women themselves. A policy which enables women to complain may also help prevent sexual harassment happening in the first place: 'no one should have to put up with sexual harassment – neither employer nor employee. Having a clear policy to deal with the problem can be the most effective preventative measure an employer can take to avoid a costly and upsetting complaint' (Employment Department 1992: 1).

Increasingly employers are adopting sexual harassment policies as well as equal opportunities policies. Ann Kelly, equal opportunities manager at British Rail, states: 'we have a sexual harassment policy because we cannot afford not to, we cannot afford to lose the staff' (1992).

An Incomes Data Services survey of employers (1992) showed that those who introduce sexual harassment policies do so for four reasons:

- to enhance equal opportunities;
- to guard against legal claims;
- to support business objectives;
- to comply with good employment practice.

As was shown in Chapter 1, not all managers have introduced policies and not all are aware of their obligations under the Sex Discrimination Act and yet incidents of harassment occur in all sectors of employment.

Allocating responsibility

Overall responsibility should rest with a named senior member of staff. Brenda Wilkinson (1991) also stresses the need for a *champion* to oversee the implementation of the policy and push it through the whole organization: 'the job of tackling the issue of sexual harassment is a job of managing change. It needs a champion or *change agent* who is not easily deflected by problems or by the need to compromise the approach in consideration of other competing priorities'.

Managers need to be told that it is their responsibility to tackle sexual harassment and take it seriously. Managers must 'own' the policy; they have a key role in setting the tone for behaviour in the organization. Employers who have put the responsibility of a sexual harassment policy wholly into the hands of a specialized officer who may not be particularly senior have achieved less than those who have used a senior officer as 'champion' and who have involved the support of all managers (WASH 1992). Management induction should include training on the sexual harassment policy, providing the opportunity for managers to assess their own values and perceptions of sexual harassment. It is also crucial that it be known that managers have a responsibility and that senior managers are taking the lead. One way this can be done is by having a foreword in the policy signed by the chief executive of the company. In one company a senior manager went round the company personally removing 'pinups' and 'girlie' calendars, thus giving a very clear message that management was associated with the policy at the very highest level. Managers should also be made aware that if they fail to take prompt action in support of the complainant when sexual harassment is brought to their attention they are failing in their duty as managers; in many organizations this itself is seen as a disciplinary offence.

Consultation with trade unions or staff representatives

Prior to developing a policy it is essential to consult and involve the workforce. This involvement, which can be done through its representatives, will give a better basis on which to build a policy and will ensure that the staff feel the policy is relevant to them. Consultations should continue throughout the development of the policy and whenever the policy is reviewed.

Writing a policy statement

All policies should contain a *policy statement* representing the organization's position on sexual harassment. A policy statement is a statement of intent, it gives the organization's commitment on sexual harassment and gives the clear message that this is behaviour the organization will not tolerate and that in the organization it is not appropriate workplace behaviour. The statement could also outline the legal situation, managers' responsibilities, the fact that sexual harassment is a disciplinary offence. It should also indicate that any complaint will be treated seriously, in confidence and with sympathy. Finally the statement should make it clear that no one will be victimized for bringing a complaint. The policy statement should be able to stand on its own separately from the policy itself.

The policy itself will contain a definition of sexual harassment and outline the procedures for dealing with sexual harassment. An example of such a statement is that used by London Underground:

> Every employee has the right to work without fear of harassment or abuse, whether on the grounds of sex, race or colour, disability, sexual orientation, or indeed any ground. Each one of us has the responsibility to protect that right. The company is committed to eliminating workplace harassment and creating a productive environment where employees are treated with dignity and respect. We have procedures in place which enable employee complaints of harassment to be dealt with promptly and fairly.

Area to be covered in a sexual harassment policy

A policy should start by giving the policy statement. With a harassment policy it is useful to draw up a code for managers and one for employees, outlining the procedure each would need to follow in cases of sexual harassment. Codes for employees should cover both advice for those who are being harassed and alleged harassers. Examples of such codes are given in Appendices 3 and 4.

Definition of sexual harassment

A policy should include a definition of sexual harassment together with illustrative examples. Some policies give the different definitions for different forms of harassment (sex, race, disability, age and so on). A definition of sexual harassment could be: offensive behaviour based on gender. The definition should also stress that the recipient's perception of the behaviour as offensive is key. Sexual harassment is not behaviour that intends to offend, but behaviour that does indeed offend the recipient. As many men do not understand what women find offensive (see the MORI survey for the GMB discussed in Chapter 1), it is useful to give examples (see also the first section of Chapter 1): verbal behaviour such as taunts, dirty jokes, unwanted sexual remarks; non-verbal behaviour such as persistent staring, pinups, pornographic material, gestures or graffiti; physical harassment such as touching, kissing or rape. Some definitions also include bullying. The London Borough of Sutton's policy defined this as 'undermining or undervaluing someone's work'.

Complaints procedures

At present in many organizations where there is no sexual harassment policy, the only recourse open to anyone complaining of sexual harassment is to use the grievance procedure. The only contact available in this case is almost always the manager. This obviously can be a problem in those instances of sexual harassment where the manager is the harasser, as often happens. This is one of the reasons why it is much better to have a separate complaints procedure for sexual harassment. Both an informal and a formal procedure should be adopted. An employee could approach a manager, an adviser or a counsellor, possibly with a friend or a trade union representative, all of whom would need training around the policy (see the section on training in this chapter). Their names, titles and phone numbers should be made known to all staff. Employees should always have the option of approaching a woman. This is rarely an option with ordinary grievance procedures where the first approach is to a manager who is almost invariably a man. Some organizations use telephone hotlines. Telephone hotlines and suggestion boxes can also be used to let managers know where there are problems that need action (e.g., pinups that need removing); in this case complaints can be anonymous. It should be possible for managers to take action against a known harasser even if no woman has complained. If someone is causing problems with the workforce, managers have a duty to respond. Some organizations specify that anyone can make a complaint, even if it is not them who is being harassed (London Borough of Sutton). Policies need to be written sensitively and in a clear and approachable style since many women are very fearful of making a complaint. If the procedure looks forbidding or complicated, a complainant may chose to leave the company rather than complain. In organizations without policies this is one of the most common outcomes of sexual harassment.

Timescales
Most employers do not set a time limit within which a complaint should be made. But whether there are time limits or not, this should be made clear in the policy. The complaints procedures should include a clear timetable so that women know how long the process will take. Once a complaint has been made it should be dealt with promptly. Ideally an initial response should be within 24 hours. While a formal complaint is being investigated it may be necessary to suspend the alleged harasser if the case appears serious. Timescales should be strictly adhered to particularly if the alleged harasser is suspended on full pay. Throughout the process the complainant should be kept informed of what is happening and be given the choice (as much as possible) on the next step. It is important for the complainant's self esteem to feel somewhat in control of the situation. All those involved, including witnesses, should be reassured that all information will be kept, as much as possible, confidential and that they will be protected from victimization.

Informal complaints
A policy should make it possible for women to make informal complaints since, as was pointed out above, most women do not want to see the harasser 'punished' but simply want him to stop. Many people who have suffered from harassment are too embarrassed to go down a formal route. In addition to this, since men frequently do not realize that their behaviour is offensive, an informal route may be the most effective way to proceed. The approach could be verbal or written. A woman should be advised to tell the harasser to stop, that she does not like the way he is

behaving, or she could ask the manager, adviser or counsellor to approach the harasser on her behalf.

If the matter is dealt with informally no records should be kept without the consent of the complainant. If records are kept they should not be placed on anyone's personal file. They should be kept in a secure place for several months and then destroyed. Information for monitoring purposes will however be kept but no employees will be identified in this process (see section on monitoring and review below). If the action becomes formal and a complaint upheld, they will be placed with the complaint on the personal file of the harasser.

The advantages of informal action are:

- it is immediate;
- it encourages women to report;
- it shares responsibility for action with the complainant.

However, informal action does not give any message to the rest of the staff that sexual harassment is being tackled and leaves the complainant open to victimization.

Formal complaints
Usually a formal complaint should be put in writing. The initial investigation could be carried out by the person to whom the complaint is made or by another manager if there is likely to be a conflict of interest.

The advantages of formal action are:

- it publicizes the organization's commitment to combating sexual harassment;
- it obliges managers to take their responsibilities seriously;
- it gives better protection to the complainant against victimization;
- it allows the organization to take action against the harasser;
- it can provide the basis for reviewing the policy.

The disadvantages of formal action are:

- it is more stressful for all;
- it is more difficult to maintain confidentiality;
- there can be hostility from other members of staff;

- it can be more difficult to collect evidence;
- the alleged harasser may get union representation often at a higher level (putting him at an advantage over the complainant who will usually be represented by a less experienced union representative).

In formal procedures, a panel of two or three people should carry out the investigation. In such cases there should be at least one women on the panel. If the complainant is black there should also be a black member on the panel since many cases of sexual harassment of black women also include a component of racial harassment.

There should also be a note-taker present, who is not seen as a member of the panel (so is impartial). Ideally the same person should be note-taker throughout the whole investigation as this is more likely to ensure consistency. After each meeting of the panel, both the complainant and the alleged harasser should be asked to sign agreed written notes of the meeting. A policy should clearly state how many days after a complaint has been made the panel will meet to interview the complainant. Complainants should be allowed to bring someone for support or to represent them (a colleague, an adviser, a trade union representative – see Chapter 6 on the role of representatives). Both sides (complainant and harasser) should be allowed to call witnesses. Witnesses should be offered anonymity and be allowed to be accompanied by a friend or union representative. The panel itself may wish to interview other staff. The panel may meet several times and recall people for interview. Indirect evidence should be sought, for example, to ascertain what happened before and after the alleged harassment. A panel can find that harassment occurred on the basis of indirect evidence alone if there are, for example, witnesses to the complainant's behaviour before and after the incidents complained of. Panels should conclude by writing a report with recommendations for action to be taken (if any). The outcome of an investigation could be that no further action is taken, that the matter is resolved informally, that the harasser is moved or that the harassment is such that disciplinary measures need to be taken. Moving the harasser is usually preferable to moving the complainant, unless the complainant herself wants to be moved. Otherwise, moving the complainant could be seen as *blaming the victim*. Moving the harasser may not always be an option, if, for example, he works in an area of speciality not found anywhere else in the organiz-ation (e.g., to where would you move a physicist from the physics department of a university?). What could be done in such cases is to put very strict constraints on his behaviour. If there is not sufficient evidence to uphold a complaint, it may still be necessary to move either the harasser or the complainant if they feel they do not want to work together. If the complaint is unproven counselling should be offered to both sides.

Once a decision has been made it is important to follow this up by checking that no victimization occurs as a result of the complaint. The situation should be monitored for a while. If the recommendation is that disciplinary action be taken, a separate panel will decide on the nature of such action (see below). This could follow the company's normal disciplinary procedure. Copies of the report should be given to the complainant and the alleged harasser. Ideally panels should aim to conclude their investigation within 30 days of a complaint being made.

Any organization should view complaints in a positive light; it shows that the policy is working and that sexual harassment is being tackled.

Malicious complaints

Some harassment policies also include a statement to the effect that anyone found guilty of a malicious unfounded complaint will be disciplined. It is important to note, however, that malicious behaviour of this kind is extremely rare. Lesley Holland, a management trainer and consultant, says:

> there is little evidence of malicious complaints but this is a powerful myth . . . A suspicion that revenge may be a motive can affect the way that people making complaints are treated. Much concern is often expressed about a 'poor harasser' who is maliciously and wrongly accused. For some investigators there is a wish to operate an 'innocent until proven guilty' approach to the investigation which can often

result in treatment of the complainant as 'a liar until the complaint is proved'.

(1994: 35)

Appeals

Appeals by both sides should be allowed within a strict timescale (for example, 30 days from the date of the panel's concluding report). Employers should be cautious about granting appeals to the alleged harasser. An appeal could put the complainant through a double ordeal, having to go through explaining what happened for a second time. There is a danger that the organization is shown to have inadequate complaints procedures if it was unable to reach an appropriate decision in the formal complaint stage. This could be a problem if the case ends up going to industrial tribunal. It could show the organization in a poor light. Many complaints procedures have an automatic right to appeal. This is not necessary if the formal stage is properly conducted; appeals should only be allowed if there are very good reasons why the first panel could not have reached the correct decision (e.g., if there is new evidence).

Disciplinary procedures

The disciplinary stage should be quite separate from the investigation by the panel. In the disciplinary process the panel and the complainant will act as witnesses for the employer in a case against the harasser.

A sexual harassment policy should make it clear that proven cases of harassment will be liable to disciplinary measures. It is important that harassers who have been shown to be guilty should be disciplined if the sexual harassment policy is going to have any credibility. In cases of harassment which are liable to be the basis of a claim by the complainant under the Sex Discrimination Act (for example, if the harasser has threatened the complainant with some action if she refuses to go out with him, or if he has made unwanted sexual advances to her), an employer would be advised to treat the case (once it has been investigated and proven) as gross misconduct. Failing this the employer could

90

be liable for unlawful discrimination (see the first section of Chapter 3).

Disciplinary measures could range from formal warnings to dismissal. It is worth noting that some cases could also result in criminal proceedings. However, managers need to bear in mind that a disciplinary hearing is not a trial.

The role of advisers

It is useful to have nominated officers who can be contacted in confidence, give support and advise on possible courses of action. Such people are often called *counsellors, advisers, listening posts* or *sympathetic friends*. If the term counsellor is used in a policy, make it clear to staff that this does not mean that these nominated people are *professional counsellors*. The advisers usually play no part in a formal complaint; at the informal stage they can give advice on how to get the harasser to stop or they can offer to speak to the harasser on the woman's behalf. If someone wants to go ahead with a formal complaint they can again advise and help in following the procedure and give support throughout the whole process. All information imparted to them should be kept confidential. Advisers should be trained in their job. They are often ordinary members of staff who are prepared to take on this additional role. In their role as advisers they must be accountable only to top management and their role as adviser must not have any adverse consequences for their position as an employee. The advisers must include women (as most cases of sexual harassment involve women being harassed). In most organizations at least half the advisers are women (Incomes Data Services 1992). An adviser should have access to a private room, a private telephone (which will not be listened into) and must herself be protected against victimization (for cases where the complaint may be against a senior manager). Some companies use the services of independent advice or counselling agencies instead of training members of their own staff for this job.

Advisers can be supported by a network within an organization. Without such a network there is evidence that the burn out rate among advisers is very high. It may happen that advisers become aware of one harasser who continually offends whilst no woman is prepared to make a formal complaint against him. This presents a dilemma: what should they do about confidentiality? In such cases advisers can try and encourage women to make a formal complaint. In one organization advisers meeting together discovered that most of them had heard complaints about the same man who had harassed 22 women. As a group, the advisers supported the women in taking action (WASH 1992). If the harasser's behaviour is putting other people in danger, then an adviser would have a duty to report it. If the harasser's behaviour is such that the employer might be taken to an industrial tribunal, then advisers should break their confidentiality and inform a senior manager. In such cases the woman must be informed of the action the adviser is going to take.

Some trade unions have objected to the work of advisers in as much as their role can mean that a potentially unlawful case of harassment can take such a long time before arriving at industrial tribunal that it is out of time (a complaint to industrial tribunal has to be made within three months of the incident to which it refers). Advisers are crucial in supporting a woman who may not otherwise make a complaint. However, advisers must be made aware of the time limits for industrial tribunal and should advise women accordingly.

Advisers should advise women to keep a diary of events, making notes of the harassment, the dates it occurs, descriptions of what happened, whether there were any witnesses and the course of action taken, in particular whether they asked the harasser to stop. Advisers can make the first set of notes on the woman's behalf. Women should be told to make a note of any future harassment and to tell the harasser that they do not like his behaviour. All this information will be important if she decides at some point to make a formal complaint.

Two examples of policies are given in Appendix 2.

Implementing a sexual harassment policy

The successful implementation of a sexual harassment policy depends on several things. Without careful implementation a policy could end up in a manager's drawer and be quite ineffective.

Managers' responsibility

Successful implementation of a sexual harassment policy, as with any equal opportunities policy, requires top management support and commitment. Brenda Wilkinson stresses this point saying that 'the organisational and strategic nature of the problems to be solved makes such top-level support imperative' (1991: 13).

Training staff and advisers

A sexual harassment policy should include a commitment to training. Training should occur before a policy is publicized, so that all is in place to implement it. All those who may be involved in upholding the policy need to be trained (designated managers, personnel officers, advisers). Training should include an understanding of why the policy is important as well as training directly on implementing the policy. Training for advisers needs to give them enough understanding of harassment and of the policy to handle cases with confidence.

Training for the rest of the staff should occur after the training of those who will deal with harassment cases. This is important since training in general is likely to raise awareness of what sexual harassment is about and therefore enable people to make complaints about behaviour they had until now tolerated as inevitable. Trained staff need already to be in place to deal with complaints.

As some employees will be reluctant to go on training, sexual harassment training should also be part of other training courses such as management courses or courses on interpersonal skills. Training concerning sexual harassment generally and the company's policy in particular should also be part of all induction training of new employees. This sort of 'awareness' training is probably the best preventative measure an organization can take against potential cases of sexual harassment (see Chapter 7 for further details).

As we saw in Chapter 3, without training a company could leave itself open to being liable for cases of harassment brought under the Sex Discrimination Act, since training is seen in law as taking reasonable steps to avoid discrimination at work.

Communicating the policy to all staff

Once a policy has been drawn up it needs to be publicized. Publicizing the policy to the workforce can be done in a number of ways. Posters can be used, articles in the company's newsletter, a summary of the policy can be put in the staff handbook, leaflets and guides/booklets outlining the policy can be distributed or announcements can be made to staff. Brighton Council put the names of their *sympathetic friends* (advisers) in the women's toilets. One organization put a message about its policy on all its internal telephone directories, another organized a series of barbecues where staff could come and burn the pinups that had been on the walls. Another company issued stickers saying 'no sexual harassment wanted in my workplace' and put them in pay packets asking the staff to stick them on anything that they felt was not acceptable; in this workplace, where most of the staff were male, stickers went up on graffiti, posters etc. All material used should address both managers, who might find themselves having to deal with a sexual harassment case, and employees who might be harassed. Information for managers needs to stress their responsibility, that sexual harassment is to be taken seriously and dealt with sensitively. Information for employees generally should stress that the organization does not condone sexual harassment and that all complaints will be dealt with promptly, contact names and phone numbers should be clearly marked. A variety of methods for disseminating information can be used at the same time, including briefings for managers, staff and trade unions. There could also be discussions around the policy at various meetings such as at induction meetings and at team meetings. Some companies have used trade unions to distribute the policy to staff. Some have also sent the policy to applicants and told them that they may be questioned on it at the interview! South London Family Housing Association incorporates sexual harassment

into their equal opportunities policy which is sent to all applicants.

Whatever strategy is used to communicate the policy, it is
important that it be linked to other policies in the organization:
the equal opportunities policy or a policy on 'quality of working
life' (British Rail did this). It is also important to relaunch the
policy at regular intervals so that its message reaches new
members of staff and is reinforced in the minds of everyone else.

Posters and leaflets can be different for managers and other
staff. For example, Hammersmith and Fulham Council put up
posters for managers saying 'No Laughing Matter: Stop Sexual
Harassment' and for other staff, 'Don't Suffer in Silence'. Each
poster also had a contact number for more information and help.
Leaflets from the same organization gave definitions of sexual
harassment, stated the Council's commitment, gave information
for women on steps to follow if experiencing sexual harassment
with the following statement on the back of the leaflet:

. . . . What to do if you are sexually harassed.

Get support;
Ask the person to stop;
Talk to your line manager;
Keep a record of what happens;
Make a formal complaint.

Remember – for years women have suffered this sort of
behaviour in silence. Now the Council's policy is there to
back you up.
Break the silence.

Another example is from another London Borough, Hounslow, where the slogan on leaflets and posters is 'Harassment is
out of order'; the leaflet states:

Hounslow Council recognises that harassment in the workplace seriously affects lives. It humiliates, offends, exploits
and undermines staff. It interferes in job performance,
creates stress at work, forces people to accept low status jobs,
denies rightful opportunities and may overlap into their
personal lives. . .It devalues a person's role as a worker and

95

makes them feel unwelcome at work. **Harassment is always serious and will not be tolerated**.

The leaflet also gives a definition of harassment, Council procedures and what to do if you are being harassed, as well as contact numbers.

Changing the culture

All the evidence shows that if a workplace is very *male*, sexual harassment is more likely to take place (see the second section of Chapter 2). Immediate action can be taken to change the workplace environment. Managers could be seen to go round removing posters and pinups. Some organizations have taken a more thorough approach; Leeds City Council moved on several fronts at once, running a seminar for chief officers and at the same time giving time off for women at the bottom of the organization to meet and discuss the policy. Out of these meetings some women offered to become contact names.

Training can be extremely effective in changing workplace culture. Some organizations have also offered assertiveness training to women staff, thus enabling them to feel empowered enough to cope with the harassment themselves. The drawback of this sort of approach is that it puts the onus on the person being harassed, away from the manager and the harasser who need to take responsibility for their own actions. To successfully change the workplace culture it is important to create an awareness throughout the organization; everyone should learn to question themselves (e.g., will this joke offend? If in doubt don't tell it) and to challenge others. People need to remember that what is acceptable in one culture (a male culture, for example) may be unacceptable in another.

One of the best ways of changing the workplace culture is to show how seriously complaints are dealt with.

Setting up monitoring, evaluation and review procedures

As with any equal opportunities initiative, monitoring of the policy is essential. Monitoring can also be used to develop and improve the policy. Evaluation and review occurs in many large organizations at the network meetings of advisers, but in any case a six monthly collation of data and review are advisable. Monitoring should be done across the whole organization and collated centrally. Those responsible for the policy should also be responsible for monitoring and review (although they can delegate the task to someone else, the overall responsibility is theirs). Some qualitative monitoring should be done every so often (every two or three years) to get a clearer measure of how the policy is perceived to be working by the employees. This would be done by face-to-face interviews or with discussion groups.

It must be remembered that when a sexual harassment policy is first introduced the number of complaints may be large and there is nothing to measure this against. After a while, if the policy is successful, the number of complaints should decrease and be mainly dealt with at the informal stage.

Monitoring should cover formal and informal complaints. The information collected should include:

- in which department/section the harassment occurred (this will enable managers to pin-point places of work where repeated harassment takes place);
- the type of harassment;
- how complaints were dealt with and resolved (this can be used to see which approaches work and which don't);
- what the response times were;
- details about the complainant (age, race, grade);
- details about the harasser (age, race, grade);
- whether the harassment was accompanied by racism or other forms of discrimination (against disabled people, lesbians and gay men, older people and other groups experiencing discrimination).

In introducing and in reviewing a sexual harassment policy, efficient implementation can be measured by performance indicators. These could take the form of checklists with dates for implementation:

- allocating responsibility;
- consultation with trade unions or staff association;
- introduction of an equal opportunities policy;
- writing a policy statement on sexual harassment;

- writing a sexual harassment policy including complaints procedures (informal and formal) and disciplinary procedures;
- appointing advisers;
- training staff (managers and advisers);
- communicating the policy to all staff;
- publicizing the policy in the workplace, addressing both potential victims of harassment, harassers and managers who may need to deal with complaints;
- setting up monitoring procedures;
- setting up review mechanisms and dates.

Conclusion

In summary, this chapter has outlined the importance of having a policy, how a policy should be developed and how it should be implemented. The chapter has reviewed a whole series of measures to be taken which will ensure that an effective sexual harassment policy is in place. Implementing some of these measures without others, for example, training staff without having a policy, will not be effective. The chapter has also stressed the importance of trade union involvement. Trade unions have been instrumental in developing and implementing sexual harassment policies. Trade unions and advice agencies are the topic of the next chapter.

6

TRADE UNIONS, THE EQUAL OPPORTUNITIES COMMISSION AND ADVICE AGENCIES

For many years, trade unions, the Equal Opportunities Commission (EOC) and voluntary organizations such as Women Against Sexual Harassment (WASH) have championed advances in equality at work and more specifically pressed for change around issues of sexual harassment. As well as campaigning, they advise, and often represent clients at industrial tribunals. This chapter looks at the role of these bodies in combating sexual harassment at work, in giving advice on representing clients through a complaint at work or on preparing for industrial tribunal.

Trade unions and sexual harassment

In the UK, trade unions have long campaigned to raise awareness about sexual harassment in the workplace. In 1983, the Trade Union Congress (TUC) produced a guide on sexual harassment, stressing the importance of trade unions taking an active role in tackling it as a workplace issue. The TUC argued that trade unions should ensure that the workplace was a place where women feel as free to work as men and that sexual harassment should be seen as a threat to job security and individual rights by creating a threatening environment at work. Sexual harassment was seen as 'a legitimate concern for trade unions' who had a duty 'to make members aware of, and sensitive to, the nature and scope of the problems involved, and to take action to prevent sexual harassment from occurring' (TUC 1983). Since the TUC published its guide, almost all trade unions have adopted national policies on sexual harassment, issued guidelines to their members and provided training.

Partnership with employers

Trade unions have been instrumental in negotiating and developing sexual harassment policies in conjunction with employers. From the employer's point of view, negotiating a policy with the trade union should provide a more effective strategy for tackling sexual harassment since in this way employers are more likely to carry the workforce with them.

In developing a policy, the employer and the union could share the process of gathering information about sexual harassment at work (e.g., surveying staff awareness and investigating the extent of the problem), they can share training to raise awareness of the issue and they can jointly negotiate a policy. The policy should acknowledge the shared role in combating sexual harassment.

At an early stage it is important to tackle traditional fears held by employers that, for instance, trade unions are 'out to get the management' and those held by trade unionists that, for example, employers are 'out to get the workers'. Successfully combating sexual harassment is in the interest of management and workers, employers and trade unions. Old attitudes of mistrust are unhelpful and need to be broken down. Employers and trade unions should work in partnership and share a vision for the way forward.

Many large employers have successfully developed and implemented policies jointly with their trade unions (e.g., BBC, British Gas, Royal Bank of Scotland – see Incomes Data Services Study 1992).

In the absence of any recognized trade union an employer should negotiate a policy with the staff association.

The TUC recommendations to trade unions

The TUC's 1983 guide, updated in 1991, makes the following recommendations:

- 'It is now widely recognized that sexual harassment is a legitimate trade union issue because it affects working conditions, health and safety at work, and the rights of women and men to equal treatment. Further, trade unions recognise that their members have a fundamental right to work in an environment free from harassment' (1991: 1).
- Trade unions should not tolerate sexual harassment within the union itself (at meetings, conferences etc.).
- Unions need to support harassed members.
- Sexual harassment complaints should be dealt with sensitively and in confidence.
- At a national level unions should ensure that their members know that sexual harassment is a trade union issue and must be taken seriously 'just as members are not expected to tolerate dangers to their health and safety, they should not have to put up with sexual harassment at work' (1991: 7).
- Individual union members found guilty of harassment should face disciplinary action.
- Unions should produce guidelines for members which should explain to those experiencing harassment and those found guilty of harassment what they can expect from the union.
- In workplaces which have trade union recognition, any complainant or alleged harasser should have the right to be represented by a member of their union.
- At a local level, unions should negotiate policies in their workplace jointly with management: 'the policy should be circulated to all employees, trainees, and job applicants. The main aim is to prevent sexual harassment, by making it plain that it is a disciplinary matter' (TUC 1991: 8). The guide goes on to recommend negotiating a joint clause to be added to any policy (even if it is an equal opportunities policy) which may already be in existence: 'The Union and Employer recognise that all employees have a right to a working environment free from sexual harassment and are committed to ensuring such harassment does not occur'.

- Unions should designate a woman member as a union officer and train her so that women members can turn to her in confidence for help.
- Individual trade union members should 'support any colleagues subjected to sexual harassment' and 'take a stand against sexist language and behaviour and pornography in the workplace' (TUC 1991: 8).

Individual unions pick up the challenge

Most unions have now published their own leaflets with guidelines on sexual harassment. Leaflets produced by unions have been mainly for officers, branches or local representatives, but many have been produced to help and advise women members experiencing harassment.

For example, NALGO (National Association of Local Government Officers, since 1993 NALGO has amalgamated with NUPE – National Union of Public Employees – and COHSE – Confederation of Health Service Employees – to form a new union, UNISON) produced leaflets for branch members, the latest of which included a definition of sexual harassment, an explanation of why it is important as an issue, and how to develop strategies to prevent sexual harassment. The leaflet specifically asks branches to 'look into their own behaviour', to appoint a woman as adviser for members and to undergo training. There is also advice on informal responses to harassment and on the need for union members to challenge their colleagues. Branches should offer representatives who could accompany women who want to confront their harasser or to speak to the harasser on their behalf. The leaflet also covers formal procedures and advice on negotiating a sexual harassment policy and procedure. It advises incorporating 'the policy into the employment contract, giving the complainant a contractual right to have the matter dealt with through agreed machinery and a right of action for breach of contract should the employer fail to use it' (NALGO 1992). The leaflet covers the use of the law and industrial tribunals. It also recommends situations where the branch may want to discipline a member who is a proven harasser. Rule 7 in the NALGO Constitution and Rules states that a member, on the recommendation of his or her branch executive committee or not fewer than 10 members of the National Executive Council, may be suspended or expelled if found guilty of conduct detrimental to the interests of the union or of unlawful discrimination. A member who is disciplined has the right of appeal.

Many unions have also published advice on collective bargaining to help their members negotiate policies at work. Other action taken by unions includes establishing networks of trained counsellors to advise and support women suffering sexual harassment.

Trade unions as employers

Trade unions, as employers, should also negotiate sexual harassment policies with their own staff's union representatives. It is customary for staff working for one particular trade union to belong to another trade union.

EC recommendations to trade unions

Because British trade unions have pioneered much of the work on sexual harassment most of what is recommended to trade unions by the EC is already standard practice within unions in Great Britain.

In its Code of Practice (see Chapter 4) the EC makes specific recommendations to trade unions. In the EC *Guide to the Code of Practice* (1993), these recommendations are reiterated with additional information to support them. The guide emphasizes the importance of having female union officials available for women who have been sexually harassed. The guide suggest that unions create a network of women members on a local, regional or national basis for women to call on when needing advice and support.

On the issue of representation, the guide stresses the importance of having a representative for the complainant of at least the same rank as the union officer representing the alleged harasser. This is not usual in the UK and would be a huge improvement on the present situation where alleged harassers are often represented by officials from head office.

The guide recommends applying disciplinary procedures to union officials who 'have abused their position of trust and power' by sexually harassing another member of the union.

On representation for both complainant and alleged harasser the guide quotes UCATT (Union of Construction and Allied Technical Trades):

> As a UCATT official, your priority is to assist and represent the victim of sexual harassment. Often the only 'evidence' will be one member's word against another. As with all grievances, you will have to make your mind up on each individual case. But if there is reasonable doubt, your job is to represent the victim.
>
> (1993: 87)

The Equal Opportunities Commission and advice agencies

The Equal Opportunities Commission and advice agencies play a crucial role in tackling sexual harassment; they offer independent advice, they do research into an area which has only recently been explored and where those experiencing harassment do not belong to a trade union, they represent the first port of call and often the only means of support.

The Equal Opportunities Commission (EOC)

The EOC was established in 1976 under the Sex Discrimination Act (SDA) 1975. Under the Act the EOC is required to do three things:

- to work towards the elimination of discrimination in employment, in education and training opportunities, in the provision to the public of goods, facilities, services and accommodation;
- to promote equality of opportunity between men and women;
- to keep the working of the Sex Discrimination Act and the Equal Pay Act 1970 under review and to propose amendments.

The EOC is given wide ranging powers under the Act to carry out these goals. As sexual harassment comes within the remit of the Sex Discrimination Act, it comes within the remit of the EOC.

The EOC can issue codes of practice (Section 56A of SDA). In its Code of Practice on the elimination of sex discrimination and the promotion of equal opportunities (published in 1985), the EOC stresses that the SDA applies to all employers in the UK, including UK-based subsidiaries of foreign companies and UK businesses from the largest to the smallest. Small businesses will require simpler procedures for dealing with equal opportunities but are still required to comply with the Act. The code stresses employers' responsibility to ensure that all within its workforce do not discriminate. It also stresses the responsibility of employees to comply with the Act. Finally it stresses the responsibilities of trade unions for collective bargaining to eliminate discrimination. Employment agencies are also mentioned in as much as they are responsible for not discriminating in placing job applicants.

The EOC gives advice to individuals suffering discrimination, including sexual harassment. It also gives advice to employers on developing policies and on training. In an information leaflet on sexual harassment, the EOC recommends that employers take all allegations of sexual harassment seriously adding 'as well as being potentially unlawful, sexual harassment can greatly impair the morale and performance of employees. It should not be assumed that complaints are made only by those who are over-sensitive' (EOC 1987). The EOC offers advice to employers on developing sexual harassment policies.

In cases of sexual harassment being taken to industrial tribunal by an individual, the EOC has the power under section 75 of the SDA to help negotiate a settlement, arrange for legal advice or representation by counsel or a solicitor or anyone else qualified to represent. The EOC can exercise these powers if the case raises a question of principle, if it is unreasonable to expect the complainant to go it alone because of the complexity or other difficulties of the case, or for any other special reason. Priority is given to cases in the area of equal pay, part time work, selection, pregnancy and sexual harassment. In 1992 two-fifths of cases brought to their attention were given advice and assistance.

In 1991 the EOC received 403 claims of sexual harassment. All of these related to employment. But the EOC does also deal with cases that relate to service delivery and has for example been supporting a case of a woman learner driver who is alleging harassment by her driving instructor.

The EOC has the power to undertake a general investigation into a particular subject without looking at the activities of specific individuals; it also has the power to establish 'named-person' investigations looking at the activities of a particular person or organization. During an investigation the EOC has the power to serve a notice on any person, requiring information to be given and documents to be produced, as well as to summon witnesses to give oral evidence. After an investigation, the EOC may make recommendations either for changes in practices (to a particular organization) or for changes in the law (to the government). If an investigation reveals discriminatory practices, the EOC has the power to require that the organization stop doing the unlawful act, that it informs the EOC of changes being made to prevent discrimination and that it informs its employees of the changes. The EOC can start a follow up investigation to ensure that its requirements are being complied with. If after five years, the organization has failed to prevent discrimination, the EOC can take out an injunction or order restraining the organization from discriminating. The EOC can also take out an injunction, independently of any investigation, if an organization has been found guilty of discrimination at an industrial tribunal within the previous five years.

Other advice agencies

Women Against Sexual Harassment (WASH)

WASH is a registered charity established in 1985 to offer free and confidential support and advice nationwide to anyone harassed at work, and to publicize the serious nature of sexual harassment. It can help find a solicitor to represent someone at industrial tribunal. It is the only organization of its kind specializing in advice on sexual harassment. Apart from help to individuals experiencing sexual harassment, WASH does research on sexual harassment, publishes information and also gives advice and training to trade unions and employers on procedure and practice for dealing with sexual harassment. WASH is made up of a group of women with legal, counselling, employment and women's rights experience who work on a voluntary basis. In recent years, WASH has dealt with increasing numbers of callers. In 1990 WASH produced an excellent manual for advice workers on sexual harassment and the law (WASH 1990).

Other organizations giving advice to those experiencing sexual harassment

City Centre Project is a London-wide project set up in 1984 to give information and advice to office workers on issues such as employment rights, health and safety at work, race and sex discrimination. A large proportion of City Centre's work is around sexual harassment, giving support and advice, doing training and giving talks to employers, trade unions and groups. City Centre does not represent clients at industrial tribunal.

Rights of Women (ROW) is a voluntary organization set up in 1975 to give free legal advice to women. ROW aims to inform women of their rights and to promote the interests of women in relation to the law. Advice is given mainly by phone, daytime and evenings. ROW does not normally undertake casework but will advise women experiencing sexual harassment, including helping them to find solicitors to prepare cases for industrial tribunal.

Law centres are becoming few and far between as more and more of them are closing following cuts in public spending. Among other things they give legal advice on sexual harassment at work and will occasionally represent someone at industrial tribunal.

Citizens Advice Bureaux also provide information to people experiencing sexual harassment at work and occasionally represent sexual harassment victims at industrial tribunal.

For all addresses of contact agencies see Appendix 6.

Representing complaints at work and preparing for industrial tribunal

This section is aimed primarily at trade union representatives but is meant also to help any other person representing a complainant going through a formal complaint or preparing for industrial tribunal. The role of the representative is different from the role of adviser as described in Chapter 5. Whereas the adviser advises and supports, the representative will act on behalf of a client in the manner described below, although in the absence of advisers being appointed by the organization a representative may have to take on some of that role as well.

Anyone acting on behalf of a complainant must make it clear to the complainant what the informal and formal procedures are and also what the procedure is for taking a case to industrial tribunal. Which route the complainant chooses to take is up to her. No pressure should be put on her to choose one route or the other. She is the one who will have to live with the consequences of her choice, not the representative. The representative's role is to help her make the appropriate choice.

In dealing with cases through a complaints procedure, representatives should ensure that a case which might go to industrial tribunal is not out of time. The time limit for putting a case to industrial tribunal is three months; if the case is taking longer to investigate at the workplace, an application to industrial tribunal should be made anyway. The application can always be withdrawn at a later date if it is resolved successfully through the complaints procedure.

Representation at industrial tribunal

For representation at industrial tribunal see the third main section of Chapter 3. Detailed advice is given in *Sexual Harassment of Women in the Workplace: A Guide to Legal Action*, a pamphlet produced by WASH in 1990. See also *How to Prepare a Case for Industrial Tribunal* by Robin Allen (1987) published by the EOC.

Representing a client through a complaints procedure

Throughout the procedure a representative should accompany the complainant to any meetings with the harasser or management and take notes at the meetings even if there is a designated note taker. This is important so that the official minutes of the meeting can be checked for accuracy.

Representatives should ensure that the woman is kept informed of what is happening and when decisions need to be made that she is given the choice to decide her own course of action. For sexual harassment cases to be resolved successfully it is crucial that women do not feel powerless during the procedure, but feel as much as possible 'in charge'.

Representatives could offer to speak to the harasser. Whichever course of action the complainant chooses she should be advised to tell the harasser that she does not like his behaviour (or get someone to tell him for her). This is important since harassment is standardly seen (and defined in law) as 'unwanted behaviour'. Unless the harasser is told that the behaviour is unwanted, he could claim that he did not know that it was not welcome and therefore it does not constitute sexual harassment.

The complainant must also be advised to keep a diary of events (even if this is not for immediate use, it will be essential for any case going through a formal complaints procedure or going to industrial tribunal). A diary should include dates, times and nature of harassment as well as details of any witnesses and their names. The diary should also include records of how she felt at the time of the harassment and should log any absence due to sickness, any reactions she had to the harasser or displayed to anyone else: embarrassment, anger and so on. She should also record from memory details of any events that took place up to the point when the diary was kept.

If the complainant visits a doctor, she must get a letter; this may be used as medical evidence of the effect the harassment had on her.

If she decides to resign from work because of the harassment, she should be encouraged to tell the employer why she is resigning. This is important if she decides to take a case to industrial tribunal for constructive dismissal (see the first section of Chapter 3), but it is also useful for the workplace since it alerts management to the fact that harassment is taking place.

Representing the alleged harasser

A union asked to represent an alleged harasser may wish to limit support to telling the member of his rights and refuse representation. For example, COHSE recommends that if an alleged harasser refuses to take union advice, he be refused representation (Marisa Howes from COHSE speaking at the Harassment Network, 2 November 1992). The Transport and General Workers Union (TGWU) in their 1987 leaflet take a stronger stance: 'the TGWU has already demonstrated that it will not support members sexually harassing other workers'. The leaflet then quotes from Sedley and Benn:

> in 1981 two women members of the TGWU working in the canteen of an engineering company complained about the behaviour of the head chef, also a TGWU member. He was dismissed by the company for sexual harassment. The man approached the union for help, and the district officer agreed to attend the appeal hearing to check that the disciplinary procedure was properly applied. The sacking was upheld and the man asked the union to support a claim of unfair dismissal. The union advised him of his rights and how to make the tribunal application. The TGWU was not, however, prepared to fight the case because the evidence of sexual harassment was overwhelming and their women members in the canteen had wanted action taken against the harasser.
>
> (Sedley and Benn 1982: 27)

Where unions have to represent an alleged harasser, trade union representatives should not resort to descriptions of the complainant's private life as a way of exonerating their member. This would amount to character assassination of another worker and is not advised by the TUC (1991: 10). If an alleged harasser is found guilty, the union may decide to discipline him under the union's rules or to withdraw union membership.

Union representation: a dilemma

A serious problem for trade unions arises when both the alleged harasser and the complainant are from the same union. Who does the union advise and represent if one union member is making a complaint against another? As the TUC guide book says,

> the union may be faced with a conflict of interest. Union rule books generally oblige the union to represent members during grievance procedures and at disciplinary hearings. Where a complaint is made by one union member against another, both could be entitled to union support.
>
> (1991: 10)

In most unions the branch will choose to represent the complainant and refer the alleged harasser to head office. The problem with this is that the alleged harasser then ends up being represented by a full time union official who has much more experience of complaints procedures and is more likely to impress employers. Unions should therefore think carefully before embarking on this approach. Some unions see sexual harassment, if proven, as a breach of membership terms (see NALGO 1992). This could mean that a union could refuse to represent a proven harasser at industrial tribunal. The Association of Cinematograph, Television and Allied Technicians (now the Broadcasting, Entertainment, Cinematograph and Theatre Union, BECTU) state in their rule book that sexual harassment is 'a specific disciplinary offence which, where proven, can result in loss of a member's ticket'.

Conclusion

Trade unions and advice agencies play a crucial role, they offer independent support and advice to both employers and employees. For employers, they can help with advice on developing and implementing policies as well as with training. For employees, they offer the only independent informed help available. Help from within an organization itself (for example from advisers) is extremely valuable but advisers are not in a position to 'represent'. In addition to this, for those experiencing harassment they will always be seen as more liable to have at heart the interests of their organization than the complainants own interests.

7

SEXUAL HARASSMENT TRAINING IN PRACTICE

One recommendation of the EC Code of Practice (see Chapter 4) is that training is essential if policies on sexual harassment are to be effective. UK case law shows that at industrial tribunal employers are seen as liable if no effort has been made to train staff in dealing with sexual harassment, and an organization that has a proper policy on sexual harassment and has implemented it with appropriate training is more likely to escape litigation (see the first section of Chapter 3). For example, in a 1990 case, an employee of the food retailer, Gateway, won her sexual harassment case against the company. The tribunal ruled that the company was responsible for the actions of her harasser who happened to be her supervisor. According to the tribunal the company had failed to take proper action to prevent the harassment. Although they had conducted a disciplinary hearing and issued a warning, they had not given guidance or training on harassment. Organizations can use outside trainers or develop their own in-house training. Small organizations can buy into training being offered by professional training organizations.

This chapter offers practical advice for people training in the field of sexual harassment whether they be equal opportunities officers, personnel officers, trade union officials or managers. It includes advice on training to raise awareness, training to develop a sexual harassment policy and training to implement a sexual harassment policy, including training for advisers. Examples of training exercises together with introductory exercises, a sample talk on sexual harassment, casework and role-play exercises can be found in Appendix 5. Material is drawn from the author's experience as a trainer in sexual harassment for employers, employee groups, trade unions and educational establishments.

Some general principles

Training at all levels will be more successful if it is undertaken jointly with the trade unions. This happens in many workplaces. For example at Lombard North Central, a finance company, the training programme on sexual and racial harassment was designed and delivered jointly by management and BIFU (Banking, Insurance and Finance Union), with most of the material and training being provided by BIFU (*Bargaining Report* 1990: 4). Such training proves invaluable when complaints and disputes around sexual harassment occur. Any training should involve the whole workforce, men and women. It must take into account the complexity of the issue, the link with sexism and the needs of complainants.

Training should aim to change behaviour rather than attitudes. If attitudes change that is all for the good and fortunately most people do change their attitudes with increased awareness of what sexual harassment is about and what its implications are. While employers cannot insist that people change their beliefs, an employer does have the right to demand a change in behaviour. The aim of the training should be to enable employees to understand that some types of behaviour are not acceptable at work and that the organization has the right to expect that certain standards of conduct be met. Across an organization, training should range from raising awareness around sexual harassment – that it is not tolerable behaviour – to understanding sexual harassment sufficiently to be able to develop a policy. Training can take several forms, from talks to workshops, videos, exercises, group discussions and role play. The more in depth the training, the more varied the training tools. In all training, handouts are essential if trainees are going to be able to refresh their memory of what they have learnt. Handouts should certainly include a copy of the company's policy, the legal situation with regard to sexual harassment, advice on how to handle a complaint and the list of contact names and numbers.

Some organizations do 'cascading' training where first one group is trained, then this group trains other groups who in turn train yet other groups and so on. Brighton Council used cascading training:

> the inspiration for this was prompted by financial constraints ... However, once thought of, the approach solved at least two other problems. First, it provided an example to 'reluctant adapters' that some managers at least support the policy. Second, it enabled the training programme to be completed in a fraction of the time that it would normally take one external training organisation to run 35–40 courses at a rate of 12 managers on each course. Speed in implementing a programme to prompt attitude change is important.
>
> (Wilkinson 1991: 12)

Awareness training in sexual harassment

Two key principles need to be decided before embarking on any training: should training be in 'women only' and 'men only' groups and should it be among employees of the same grade? The advantage of having training in women-only groups during awareness training is that women are more likely to feel able to talk about their experiences and develop strategies to cope and challenge sexual harassment at work. In mixed groups women feel inhibited and profit less from the training. Once an awareness has been reached and training is aimed at developing and implementing a policy, training in mixed groups works well. In women-only groups, it does not seem to make much difference whether women are from different grades, they still all share the experience of being women. This is the most relevant point in discussing sexual harassment. If groups are of mixed gender it may be easier to have groups of employees roughly of the same grade as this reduces the power imbalance of the group and should free up discussion.

Awareness training can be as short as two hours but ideally should be half a day (three and a half hours). Those who have never had any training on equalities issues will often feel very nervous or very threatened. An exercise to break the ice at the start of the training will deal with these fears. This could be done by asking people to break up into pairs and discuss with each other where they work and what they hope to get out of the training, or discuss with each other an example of possible sexual harassment answering a set of pre-set questions (see sample questionnaire in Appendix 5). After these exercises trainees can be brought together for an open-ended discussion on their feelings about sexual harassment. I often hold a brainstorming session addressing a general question such as: 'what do you think sexual harassment is?' or 'do you think sexual harassment is a problem for this organization?'. With a very hostile group this exercise takes time, but it is crucial as it allows the training, which could otherwise be blocked, to continue.

Each organization should plan its own awareness training according to its own requirements. Groups should ideally be of up to 15 people, preferably with two trainers. Two trainers make the training more interesting and mean that the training is more effective since trainers are less likely to get tired. A pattern for awareness training I have found effective is as follows (examples of exercises to accompany the sessions below can be found in Appendix 5):

1 introductory exercise (anything from 15 minutes to an hour);
2 talk by trainer on what sexual harassment is (20 minutes to half an hour). This should give the theoretical and legal framework. If the training session covers more than half a day, it would be better to separate the theoretical and legal framework, followed by different exercises on each;
3 exercises in small groups of three to five people with each group working on cases to learn to apply what has been understood under the previous step (15 to 20 minutes). Alternatively members of each group can be asked to role play;
4 a plenary session where each of the small groups can report

back and the larger group as a whole can share its experience
and understanding (30 minutes);
5 a final open session to decide where the group (and individuals) should go from here (what has been gained and what can
be taken away from the training).

The discussion about the definition of sexual harassment, if
aimed at managers should include reference to the fact that
tolerating sexual harassment in any organization costs money in
terms of increased turnover, reduced productivity (Chapter 1)
and possible litigation (Chapter 3). Somewhere there should be
mention of the different perceptions men and women have of
sexual harassment. Men see much of sexual harassment as
flirtation and see it as less of a problem than women do (see
Chapter 1). Men need also to understand that jokes that seem
funny to them may be offensive to women. Where there is more
extensive awareness training, this can also include exercises on
understanding sexism, given that sexual harassment is a form of
sexism (see Chapter 2).

As an alternative to giving a talk in session 2, a video can be
shown, followed by a discussion to bring out the main theoretical
elements for an understanding of sexual harassment. A good
video would be one with which a group of trainees can identify
and that covers the issues a trainer wants them to discuss. One of
the best videos for training in sexual harassment is *A Costly
Proposition*. This American video has five sketches, each representing a different situation. It is available from 'Symposia' (a
training organization based in Oxford, telephone number – 0865
750008). Many videos are outdated in terms of practice, legal
issues and work situations. Many also do not portray representative workforces, for example, they are all 'white' and 'able-
bodied'. Good videos are rare and often very expensive to hire. A
list of usable videos is available from the EOC. Videos can be
bought from the Institute of Personnel Management, the EOC,
the TUC and the BBC (addresses are given in Appendix 6).

Training to develop a sexual harassment policy

Training to develop a sexual harassment policy usually takes from half a day to a day, depending on how developed the organization's equality work is. The role of the trainer will be different from that in awareness raising. Here the trainer works to enable the trainees to develop a policy relevant to their organization. The trainer needs to use the trainees' knowledge of their own workplace and enable them to develop a policy that meets the needs of the organization and its workforce. If a policy is to be successful, it is important for the group to work out what is needed for the particular organization they work for. This ensures that the policy is appropriate to the organization and that those who have power in the organization (managers, personnel and unions) *own* the final result. There should be no more than 15 people in a training group. Trainees should include managers, personnel officers, trade union officers and representatives of any equalities committee or women's group. Women should not be in the minority in the group or they risk feeling too intimidated to participate constructively.

The trainees should already have an awareness of sexual harassment and have undergone the sort of awareness training mentioned earlier in this chapter. To develop a sexual harassment policy, the group will need to cover at least the following issues:

- why a policy is necessary (this will recap on the awareness issues);
- what the policy needs to contain;
- what the complaints procedure should be and how it fits in with any existing complaints procedures;
- what disciplinary procedures should apply and whether the existing ones are adequate.

From my experience, a sample half day training session might be:

1 Why have a sexual harassment policy? Brainstorming session (half an hour or more depending on trainees' awareness) which should include the advantages to the organization of having a policy in terms of staff welfare and increased efficiency, the need to avoid litigation and the cost to the organization of not having a policy. This session could also look at policies already in place such as those on equal opportunities or racial harassment.

2 The next session would be on developing a sexual harassment policy. Trainees should be in groups of three or four, each working on one of the main characteristics of a policy: the statement, how to investigate a complaint (informal action, formal action), disciplinaries, the role of advisers, the importance of confidentiality. Each small group should decide on the bare bones of what is needed in a statement, a complaints procedure and so on. This can be done by looking at models or examples from other organizations and adapting them accordingly. The length of this session varies greatly; amongst more experienced trainees it may take 20 to 30 minutes, in some instances it will take much longer.

3 At a plenary session each group could report back and the whole group discuss each others findings (this plenary could last an hour). Recommendations for a policy would be written on a flipchart so that there can be no misunderstanding and so that they can be taken away for future use. The group would then give its recommendations to someone chosen to draw up the draft policy at a later stage after the training.

4 In the next session, time would be spent seeing how the suggested policy would be applied in practice; the recommendations on the flipchart would need to be available for reference. Small groups could work on different cases, asking themselves in the light of the draft policy, what would you do as an employee suffering harassment, as a manager, as a personnel officer, as a trade union representative? (examples from Appendix 5 could be used in this exercise). The aim of this session is to see if the policy is sufficient to cope with the likely situations.

5 This could be followed by another plenary session where the small groups report back on any difficulties encountered in applying the draft policy.

6 In a full day's training there would be time for a further session spent writing up the draft policy, on the basis of the recommendations, with each group working on one aspect of the policy. For this session groups could use again sample policies to see if anything new needs to be added. Sample policies could include the EC Code of Practice, recommendations from the UK government, the Institute of Personnel Management and

actual policies from other organizations (see particularly Chapters 4 and 5).

7 In a final session the group should decide what action needs to be taken to get the policy agreed, get it implemented and get it known. The group may decide that a further training session would help, and a half day session for such is outlined below. Alternatively the training may already have been scheduled to take up two half days, one on developing a policy and one on implementing it. If this option is followed, it is best for the gap between the sessions to be a week as this will allow trainees to digest the information they have received and think further upon it. The learning process continues between sessions.

Training for implementing a sexual harassment policy

This training can either be combined with the session on developing a sexual harassment policy or be run separately. Training aims to enable trainees to develop strategies for implementing an agreed policy. Ideally, if run as a separate training course, participants should be those in the organization who will be responsible for implementation. Training may be needed if a policy has been developed but never implemented, a paper exercise with no real change in the workplace. This training could take half a day to a day depending on the needs and resources of the organization.

A sample half day training could be as follows:

1 The training would start with an introductory session of half an hour on what harassment is. It is important to recap in this way even for those who have had previous training. This session could be done either through a general discussion or by asking trainees to pair up and discuss the issue for five or ten minutes then report back to the group. Obviously this introduction will not be necessary if it is part of, and run on the same day as, the training to develop a policy outlined previously.

2 A second session could be spent going through the organization's policy, looking at its content and procedures. This would probably last half an hour and could simply be a talk by

the trainer or by small groups of trainees reading through different aspects of the policy, highlighting the main points and reporting back to the main group. Even for those who have just gone through a training session on developing a sexual harassment policy, it may be useful to have a short summary of decisions made, stressing the main aspects of the policy.

3 Groups could then be asked to look at what they thought the barriers would be to implementing the policy. This could be a session where trainees are paired for five to ten minutes and then the main points are pooled in a plenary session.

4 Once the key problems of implementation are identified, the group can split up into small groups of three or four to work on ways of tackling them. These may include: communicating the policy (publicity), training the workforce, monitoring and reviewing the policy, commitment from senior managers and their role in promoting the policy, problems faced by advisers, problems around confidentiality, the role of trade unions. Each small group should be given at least 15 to 20 minutes to work on these issues. Time needs to be allowed for groups to report back to the plenary (five minutes for each small group).

5 The trainees should then be 'reshuffled' into a new set of small groups and given sample exercises to allow people to assess what has been learnt from the previous sessions and to see how the policy might work in practice. The trainees would need to ask themselves questions like 'what would you as a manager/ co-worker/trade unionist/adviser, do in this situation?' Each group is asked to answer these questions as they relate to a particular example. If implementation training follows straight after policy development training this session is unnecessary. But if the two sessions are separated by a period of time (say a week), or are being done with a different group, then this session is worthwhile. It often helps if trainees also practice taking on the roles of manager, co-worker, adviser. Such role play would give people the context within which to use the skills learnt in the training session. In role play there could also be an observer (or the whole group could observe) who could comment on what was helpful by way of questions from the manager/adviser/panel and what acted as a barrier for the woman bringing a complaint. Alternatively groups can role

play, advising a woman complaining of harassment, dealing with a colleague harassing others, being in a panel investigating a complaint etc. At the end of this session the group can share their experiences in a general discussion. Role play is tricky as a training tool and many trainers do not feel comfortable with it. It is better not to use it if the trainer feels unsure.

6 A final session could look at 'where we go from here'. This would define the actions that need to be taken by the group to ensure that the policy is implemented as well as actions individuals feel they might wish to take if they feel personally that it is important to challenge, rather than collude, with the prevailing workplace culture.

Training for advisers

Successful sexual harassment policies demand a network of staff prepared to act as support and give advice to women facing harassment. Giving such support is not easy, however, it requires skill and training. It requires a thorough understanding of the organization's policy and procedures on sexual harassment. It requires an understanding of the law. Some of these understandings can be acquired through the training mentioned above. But there is also a need for some specialist training, a discussion of which follows.

An example of harassment-adviser skills training comes from Shell UK (Incomes Data Services, 1992: 6). The adviser's training included: what is harassment?, case study discussion, rights of the aggrieved and the perpetrator, information gathering (emotion v. fact), working with anger and aggression, intervention and assertiveness skills, counselling skills and support systems for advisers. Other organizations have used cascading training for training their advisers. British Gas, for example, chose their advisers from existing employees who have received initial harassment training. The first advisers received two days training from an external consultant then selected other staff to become advisers and trained these themselves. Most of their advisers are in personnel but some come from other parts of the workforce (Incomes Data Services 1992).

Training for advisers must include the following:

- an understanding of sexual harassment (if not previously trained);
- an understanding of the organization's harassment policy;
- an understanding of the complaints procedure and disciplinary procedure;
- an understanding of the role of the adviser. Whose side is the adviser on? What specifically is his or her role? To fully understand their role advisers will need to know what the task involves (advice and support) and what its limits are. An adviser should not have an investigatory role and should only take action in exceptional circumstances such as, for example, where the organization could be legally liable if the adviser failed to act;
- an understanding of possible dilemmas (e.g. when several women confide that the same man is harassing them: see Chapter 5 on the role of advisers);
- listening skills;
- an understanding of the importance of confidentiality;
- an understanding of the effects of sexual harassment on the health of those who experience it.

To be effective training should include casework (see Appendix 5) and role play, each trainee taking it in turn to be the 'adviser' and the person seeking advice.

Conclusion

As well as the various training mentioned above, an organization might feel the need for more in-depth training. This could be needed if, for example, particular problems are discovered through monitoring the sexual harassment policy. For example, monitoring might show that one particular department has many more cases than others or that overall few cases are being resolved at the informal stage, or that few cases are being reported (this would be an indication of people's hesitation in coming forward, possibly through lack of confidence in the organization dealing seriously with the issue). Monitoring will identify most problems and training can be provided to overcome them.

Policies need to be flexible to take account of changes in legislation, changes in the workforce or the nature of the work and changes in practice. As policies change, up-date training may be necessary.

Large organizations usually develop their own training packages and have in-house trainers. Small organizations will need to buy in training from outside consultants or send staff on courses provided elsewhere. To find outside consultants or trainers, contact Women Against Sexual Harassment, the Equal Opportunities Commission, the Institute of Personnel Management, the Industrial Society, Industrial Relations Services or voluntary organizations such as City Centre (addresses are given in Appendix 6). Most of these organisations also have training material (case studies etc.) which can be used by other trainers.

APPENDIX 1
EXAMPLE OF AN EQUAL
OPPORTUNITIES POLICY[1]

Equal opportunity in ICI in the UK (issued in 1990)

1 Policy statement

ICI believes that every employee should be treated with the same respect and dignity. It values the rich diversity and creative potential that men and women, with differing backgrounds and abilities, bring to its business community, and wishes positively to encourage a culture of equal opportunities for all, in which personal success depends on personal merit and performance.

To this end there will be no discrimination against any person for any reason that is not relevant to the effective performance of their job; all judgements about people for the purposes of recruitment, development and promotion will be made solely on the basis of their ability and potential in relation to the needs of the job.

Every employee will be fully informed and trained to do their immediate job, and have the opportunity to develop further both as a person and to pursue career opportunities consistent with their abilities.

Every manager is accountable for ensuring that this policy is actively pursued and put into practice.

2 *The prevention of sexual harassment*

ICI has a separate statement on sexual harassment.

3 *Assurance of equal treatment in recruitment, development and promotion*

Managers will be required to re-examine their procedures and systems of recruitment, potential appraisal and promotion in the light of the equal opportunities policy statement. They should contain no element of unfair discrimination, and provide encouragement to those candidates of either sex or from any background who have the necessary ability and potential.

Every individual should seek to identify their own career aspirations and be prepared to invest time and effort in pursuing them.

4 *Making equal opportunity part of training activities*

Equal opportunity should be a component in the training of all managers and employees. Managers should also consider conducting surveys or other means to raise awareness of equal opportunities problems and opportunities.

Special skills training for women for promotion or transfer to non-traditional jobs should also be examined.

5 *Establishing objectives for improvement*

Managers will be required to set themselves realistic objectives to improve the representation of women at various levels and in the various functions of the organization.

6 *Improved maternity leave, career break arrangements and related matters*

Maternity leave
The Company will pay the equivalent of full salary (less State

Maternity Pay) for the period that State Maternity Payment is payable, to those women who return to work after maternity leave, and stay in employment continuously for three months. This payment will be made in the form of a lump sum at the end of the three month period following return to work.

This new arrangement for paid maternity leave for up to 18 weeks supplements the arrangements for extended maternity leave announced last year. It will apply to staff with two years service and be operative from January 1st 1991.

Career breaks
The Career Break arrangements introduced last year should be made more generally available to staff with a good record of performance.

In addition, from January 1991, on return to work staff will be given the option of the period of the Career Break being counted for pension purposes. If a person chooses to have the period taken into account they will be required to repay the equivalent of their Pension Fund contributions for the period of the Break. In order to help them do so the Company will provide an interest free loan repayable over five years. The Company will pay its contributions in full.

Related matters
At local level Businesses should ensure that the availability of Career Breaks for men and women are well publicized, together with information about leave arrangements for fathers when children are born.

'Keeping in touch' arrangements for women on maternity leave together with 'networking' arrangements for when they return after childbirth should be developed.

7 A flexible approach to working hours and part-time working

Managers should actively encourage the development of the flexible organization of working hours, and non-traditional patterns of work, such as job sharing and term-time only working, so as to help parents combine bringing up a family with pursuing a career.

The Company confirms that reporting arrangements made necessary by the Company's Act should not be seen as an inhibition to the employment of part-time employees, and also that ICI terms and conditions, including membership of the Pension Fund, are open to part-time employees on a pro-rated basis.

8 Developing childcare provision

Managers should, in each location, ascertain the needs of employees with children to establish how they match up with the availability of appropriate community facilities. Businesses may consider giving help to establish crèches locally where there are inadequate existing facilities and there is a business need and justification.

9 Providing information and guidance

Information and guidance about the Company's equal opportunity policy and practice will be published both centrally and locally.

At national level the Company will produce a booklet clarifying its policies, practices and schemes for the purpose of communication to potential recruits and existing employees.

At local level a comprehensive set of information relevant to family and childcare should be available in each location about, for example, State Benefits, nursery places, childminding and play schemes.

10 Clarity of roles and accountability

Every employee can expect to be treated with dignity and without unfair discrimination. Equally every employee is responsible for behaving in a way which avoids unfair discrimination in the workplace.

Line managers are accountable for ensuring that the Company's positive equal opportunity policy, and the practical measures contained in this note are put into practice in their areas of responsibility.

In addition each Business should identify a senior manager with overall responsibility for progressing equal opportunity issues.

Equal opportunity should be a regular agenda item for local joint consultation meetings.

Note

1 This is not meant to be a 'model' policy.

APPENDIX 2
EXAMPLES OF SEXUAL
HARASSMENT POLICY AND
GENERAL HARASSMENT POLICY[1]

Below are two sample policies reproduced in their entirety. One is from the University of Central Lancashire – specifically on sexual harassment – and one is from London Buses Ltd – on harassment in general. Each policy is standard in the sense that similar policies can be found in many organizations.

University of Central Lancashire (1992): Sexual harassment policy

1 The University's views on equal opportunities

The University of Central Lancashire is concerned to foster an environment in which students, staff and those associated with University activities can work or study effectively. Unwanted behaviour of any kind is regarded as unacceptable and the University is particularly concerned to eliminate sexual harassment, i.e., *unwanted* behaviour of a sexual nature, or behaviour which is based on the recipient's gender or sexuality, which is offensive to the recipient.

Different kinds of situations can produce different experiences of sexual harassment and differences in attitudes and cultures can mean that what is perceived as sexual harassment by one person may not be seen as such by another. However, the common link is that the behaviour is unwanted by the recipient. The University is concerned to develop an environment in which all individuals can operate effectively, confidently and competently without harassment.

2 *Sexual harassment policy statement*

The Sexual Harassment Policy Statement is derived from the Mission Statement and associated aims.

2.1 The University seeks to provide an environment free from sexual harassment, intimidation and victimization.

2.2 All students and staff and those visiting the University premises, for example, as visitors or contractors, and anyone acting on behalf of the University will respect the rights of others and *will refrain from*:

- unwanted physical conduct of a sexual nature, such as unwanted touching or invasion of personal space;
- unwanted verbal conduct of a sexual nature, such as unwelcome sexual advances and pressure for social activity, and suggestive remarks, innuendos or lewd comments;
- unwanted non verbal conduct of a sexual nature, including sexually suggestive gestures and leering, the display, storage or transmission of pornographic or sexually suggestive pictures, objects, written or other materials, etc.;
- conduct that denigrates, ridicules, intimidates or abuses an individual because of her/his sex or sexuality, such as derogatory or degrading remarks or insults which are gender-related, or offensive comments about appearance or dress;
- abuse of power relations such that individuals receive unfair treatment based on gender or sexuality.

2.3 All line managers will be held responsible for eliminating sexual harassment of which they are aware, or should be aware, and all incidents must be reported to the Chair of the Sexual Harassment Panel.

2.4 All individuals will be held personally accountable for their actions and behaviour in cases of complaint of sexual harassment.

Under this policy the University will follow the procedure outlined overleaf in case of complaint or appeals against complaint. The University takes a serious view of sexual harassment and such behaviour may result in disciplinary action.

Brian Booth
Rector

Sexual harassment complaints procedure

(a) A member of the University who believes that s/he is the subject of sexual harassment should, if possible and in the first instance, ask the person responsible to stop the harassing behaviour. If this is not possible for any reason, or the harassment continues, or if it stops but the recipient feels that s/he would like advice or support, s/he should not hesitate to use Section (b) of this procedure.

 The Rector may take action to stop the harassment immediately and prevent its recurrence. If relocation is necessary, the Rector will seek to relocate the harasser.

(b) A panel has been appointed by the University's Equal Opportunities Committee to act as the first point of contact in issues relating to sexual harassment and to carry out preliminary investigations where necessary. Anyone wishing to seek advice or clarification about sexual harassment (whether line managers or others) or wishing to make a complaint, should contact the Chair of this Panel. The Panel consists of both male and female members of staff, including a female chair, who may act on behalf of the Panel when appropriate. The Panel will include a student representative where appropriate. The Chair will present the findings and recommendations arising from the preliminary investigations to the Rector, and will make general reports to the Equal

Opportunities Committee. The role of the Panel is advisory and it does not instigate disciplinary action.

(c) All complaints will be handled in a timely manner. All steps will be taken to maintain confidentiality as far as is consistent with progressing the complaint. If appropriate, a complaint may be resolved through mediation. Both the alleged harasser and the complainant shall be entitled to representation.

(d) If a complaint is upheld, the appropriate Staff or Student Disciplinary Procedure will be used.

(e) Anyone seeking advice, making a complaint or assisting in an investigation shall be offered support and protected against victimization or discrimination.

(f) Making a false allegation with malicious intent may result in the disciplinary procedure being invoked.

(g) A preliminary investigation by the Panel will not necessarily depend on the ability of an individual to sustain a complaint.

Sexual harassment appeals procedure

Any party directly involved in a complaint, who is dissatisfied with the processing of the complaint, may appeal within three weeks of being notified of the outcome, to the University Secretary whose decision will be final.

Brian Booth
Rector[2]

London Buses Limited (1992): Workplace harassment policy

London Buses fully supports the rights and opportunities of all people to seek, obtain and hold employment without discrimination.

Workplace harassment is a form of discrimination. It may be unlawful behaviour contrary to equal opportunities legislation. It is also improper and inappropriate behaviour which lowers morale and interferes with work effectiveness.

It is London Buses' policy to provide a productive working environment free of harassment, intimidation and victimization on the basis of sex, race, colour, disability, sexual orientation or any other personal characteristic. The company is committed to ensuring that its employees are treated with dignity and respect.

Conduct which leads to the harassment of another employee is not acceptable and will render the individual responsible liable to disciplinary action.

Definition

Workplace harassment is regarded as any conduct related to sex, race, colour, disability, sexual orientation or any other personal characteristic which is unwanted by the recipient.

It refers to behaviour that is unsolicited, unwanted and fails to respect the individual. It may be persistent or an isolated incident and may be directed towards one or more individuals. It may come from a member of staff or from the public in the course of one's duties. Whatever is its origin, harassment is behaviour which is inappropriate in an effective working environment and can result in the recipient feeling threatened, humiliated, patronized or disadvantaged.

The 'workplace' is defined as any place where the business of London Buses is conducted.

Workplace harassment may be:

Physical – including unnecessary touching, gesture or assault.
Verbal – including unwelcome remarks, suggestions and propositions, malicious gossip, jokes and banter based on sex, race or other personal characteristics.
Non verbal – offensive literature or pictures, graffiti.

Duties of supervisors and managers

All supervisors and managers are responsible for eliminating any harassment or intimidation of which they become aware, whether or not it is brought formally to their attention. Failure to do so will be considered a failure to fulfil all of their responsibilities.

Duty of employees

All employees have a duty to comply with this policy and ensure that their colleagues are treated and treat others with dignity and respect.

Harassment complaint procedure

Workplace harassment is not acceptable under any circumstances in London Buses.

Victims of harassment may be discouraged from taking action by their fear of retaliation, embarrassment or feelings of guilt.

If the work environment is to change it is essential that harassment is acknowledged and dealt with appropriately.

1 Informal action
   - An employee who believes that she or he has been the subject of harassment should first inform the harasser that their behaviour is unwelcome and ask them to stop.
   - An employee may also choose to raise the matter informally with their employing manager.
   - Advice and assistance regarding harassment may be sought from London Buses Equal Opportunities Unit and LT Counselling Service.

2 Formal action
   If the harassment persists or if the incident is considered to be serious, the recipient has the right to complain and pursue the matter in accordance with the London Buses' grievance procedure. The process is outlined below.
   (i) An employee who believes that he or she has been the subject of harassment should report the alleged act to his or her employing manager or personnel manager.
   (ii) All complaints will be dealt with quickly and in confidence. Employees shall be guaranteed a fair and impartial hearing. Both the complainant and the accused shall be entitled to trade union representation.

(iii) If the investigation reveals that the complaint is valid, prompt action will be taken to stop the harassment immediately and prevent its recurrence. If relocation proves necessary, every effort will be made to relocate the harasser and not the victim.

(iv) Employees shall be protected from intimidation, victimization or discrimination for making a complaint or assisting in an investigation. Retaliating against an employee for complaining about harassment is a disciplinary offence.

This policy is fully supported by London Buses trade unions.

(signed)

Managing Director

Notes

1 These are not meant to be 'model' policies.
2 The policy of the University of Central Lancashire has recently been amended to include other forms of harassment.

APPENDIX 3
CODE OF PRACTICE FOR MANAGERS FOR DEALING WITH SEXUAL HARASSMENT COMPLAINTS

Faced with a complaint a manager has a duty to respond. If the response is to say to women that they should put up with the behaviour, or deal with it themselves in some way, or simply avoid meeting the harasser on their own, this would count against an employer at an industrial tribunal since it would show that the employer has done nothing to stop the harasser.

When investigating a complaint, a manager needs to be aware of the importance of confidentiality. Managers cannot, however, provide unconditional confidentiality if they are to fulfil their managerial role. There will be times when a manager may need to break the confidentiality to take action against a known harasser. This would occur when a company might find itself legally challenged if action is not taken. If this proved necessary all parties should be informed of the action the manager is going to take. Apart from such rare occasions, anyone investigating a complaint should keep all information, files and documents confidential. Nothing should be kept on an employee's personal files. Breaches in confidentiality (apart from exceptions mentioned above) should be treated as a disciplinary offence.

When a complaint is brought to a manager, appropriate action needs to be taken, after listening to the complaint the manager needs to decide whether the situation should be resolved informally or formally. In this, it is important to be guided by the complainant's wishes. If she wishes to make a formal complaint, then she needs to write a statement, outlining what has happened and what she is complaining about. The statements should wherever possible include dates, times, witnesses, factual descriptions of the events, how she felt at the time, who she spoke to about the incidents and whether she told the harasser to stop. If she kept a diary, writing the statement will be relatively straightforward.

Investigations should be fair to both sides: the person bringing the complaint and the alleged harasser. Both need to be told of the procedure and the timescale for the investigation. Investigations of formal complaints should be conducted by a panel.

At the first meeting of the panel, the complaints procedure should be explained to the complainant. She should be encouraged to speak freely. Many women are very embarrassed about their experience. The panel should listen attentively to the answers and not interrupt her once she has started speaking.

The panel should avoid *blaming the victim*. Questions asked by the panel should be phrased in such a way that the complainant feels safe to talk and not under *attack*. Questions need to elicit factual information, not personal details relating to the complainant. The sort of questions which need to be asked include:

What happened?
Did he touch you?
Were there any witnesses?
Did you tell him to stop?
How did you react?
When and where did incidents take place?
Did others incidents occur?

Did you mention this to anyone at the time?
Did you make any notes?
Has your work been affected?

Stereotypes must be avoided at interview; don't assume that all women being harassed *asked for it* or that they have imagined it (they are too old, too ugly), that all harassers are office Romeos or blue collar staff. Don't ask questions which victimize the complainant: What were you wearing? Don't you think you were overreacting? Was he not joking? Why didn't you tell him to leave off?

The alleged harasser also needs to be told the process; he needs to be told of the complaint against him. The type of questions which should be asked include:

Were you aware of these allegations?
If yes, how?
Were you aware of the incident at the time?
What happened?
Did you realize that it was unwelcome?
Has the complainant spoken to you about the incident?
What did she say?
What was your reaction?

The possible outcome of the investigation needs to be made clear to both parties. As a result of the investigation, the panel needs to reach a decision based on the evidence put before it. The decision could be to move the harasser; it could also be to take disciplinary action. If moving the harasser, his new post should be of comparable pay and conditions, otherwise the harasser may have a case of constructive dismissal against the organization. Decisions will often be difficult since they may largely rest on the credibility of each party. When deciding on any action, the panel needs to assess whether the behaviour was unwelcome; the panel should take into account the 'intent' of the harasser, whether the harassment was repeated over a period of time, how severe it was, whether there had been complaints against the harasser previously, the harasser's position in the organization (was he in a position of trust or authority?) and the effect of the harassment on the victim.

APPENDIX 4
CODE OF PRACTICE FOR EMPLOYEES[1]

If you are being harassed you should do the following:

1 Keep a written record of all incidents

Note the dates, time and place, the nature of the harassment, any witnesses. Make a note of all incidents that occurred prior to you beginning the written record, with as much detail as you can remember.

2 Decide who you want to support you

Speak to the person causing offence if you feel able to. Otherwise get support by contacting one of the following:

- your manager/supervisor;
- another manager/supervisor;
- a trade union representative;
- a personnel manager;
- a manager/supervisor immediately above your own;
- a colleague;
- a counsellor in the personnel department.

3 *Give your support person full details of the events*

Decide with them what action you wish to take. With their support you may wish to:

- speak to your own manager/supervisor;
- speak to the person harassing you;
- ask them to speak to the person harassing you;
- take no action;
- lodge a formal complaint.

If you decide to do the second or third options above:

- arrange to see the harasser in a place that is confidential;
- tell them you find their behaviour offensive. Do not be apologetic. Just ask them to stop their offending behaviour. Do not give the names of any witnesses.

It is important that you are brief, factual and do not attempt to argue the rights and wrongs of the case. The purpose of the meeting is solely to tell the harasser that you find his behaviour offensive and to ask him to stop.

4 *If the harassment continues you may feel that you want to take out a formal complaint*

Consult your support person and follow the complaints procedure.

If you are accused of harassment you should do the following:

- listen to what is being said;
- understand that your behaviour is causing offence and is therefore unacceptable;
- ensure that the behaviour stops.

You will know that your behaviour is causing offence if an approach is made to you by the person who feels that you are harassing them or by someone on their behalf. This could be:

- your own line manager/supervisor;
- another manager/supervisor;
- a personnel manager;
- a colleague of the person who feels harassed;

- an employee counsellor in the personnel section;
- a trade union representative.

What happens then:

- they will ask to meet you in a place that is confidential;
- the aggrieved employee may be accompanied by another person, for support, who will act as an observer and make written notes of what is said at the meeting;
- the aggrieved employee or her representative will give full details of your behaviour which is causing offence, describe the effect it has on them and ask you to stop.

You may not have been aware that your behaviour has caused offence to this employee and you may wish to ask questions to help you to understand the other person's feelings. However it is important that you are brief, factual and do not attempt to argue the rights and wrongs of the case.

The aim of the meeting is for you to be made aware of your offending behaviour and to appreciate that your behaviour is causing harassment of the other person and is therefore unacceptable and must stop.

The harassment procedure does not allow you to take out a formal grievance against the aggrieved employee (or their representative) for raising this matter with you.

Note

1 This is loosely based on the guidance given in the Model Harassment Policy issued by the Association of London Authorities in 1993.

APPENDIX 5
TRAINING EXERCISES

Sample introductory questionnaire and exercises

To break the ice and get a group starting to think around sexual harassment, trainees can be set the following questionnaire to answer individually, in pairs or in small groups. After completing the questionnaire ask the trainees how many of these examples describe sexual harassment and how many of the statements are true. Some of the questions could be used singly as a focus for discussion in small groups (for a discussion you could also use the quotations mentioned below under 'role play').

Which of the following would you count as sexual harassment?

1 When Indira complained about the 'girlie' posters/calendars on the wall, she was told she was jealous of their bodies.
2 Mark said that Sarah had no sense of humour when she objected to a smutty joke.
3 Every morning when Leilah arrived for work, John commented on her clothes and appearance.
4 When Pat complained to her boss that Leroy was always touching her he asked her whether she enjoyed it.

5 Yasmin asked the director how he liked his coffee. He answered: 'Sweet, like you darling'.
6 The women in the office complained to the manager about the lewd language used by the men.
7 Grace got upset when the men wolf whistled at her.

In fact all the above could be describing sexual harassment.

Are the following true or false?

1 Sexual harassment is another term for flirtation.
2 It is only a bit of fun.
3 Harassment should really be taken as a compliment.
4 It is only a problem for pretty women.
5 Why all the fuss, it doesn't do any harm.
6 If you ignore the harasser, he will soon stop.
7 Sexual harassment is a private affair between employees.

All these statements are false.

Trainees can also be asked to discuss in pairs or small groups what they believe sexual harassment to be. After this exercise see if the views of women differ from those of men.

Summary of sample talk on understanding sexual harassment

Start by showing how common a problem sexual harassment is. Use the surveys mentioned in Chapter 1. Stress that the question is not whether sexual harassment exists in an organization but rather to what extent it exists. The problem is often invisible. People need to be made aware of it for sexual harassment to become visible.

Explore some of the myths around sexual harassment. Many are contained in the exercise mentioned above and if this exercise has been done, you will know which myths hold with your audience. Particularly cover myths such as: women ask for it, it is flirtation, it is part of the nature of things, it is an attempt at initiating sex, it is only a problem for pretty women. Use statistics or examples to show that these are myths and clearly not true.

Outline what sexual harassment is: unwanted behaviour as

144

perceived by the recipient. Talk about the different perception men and women have of behaviour/jokes/images; talk about the fact that different women also have different perceptions of the same behaviour/joke/image. Stress the fact that sexual harassment undermines and damages women's confidence in themselves as workers, that it emphasizes a person's gender over their role as a worker. Jokes tend to imply that this person or this type of person (e.g. *women*) are not to be taken seriously and are simply objects of fun. Sexual harassment implies that you are judged by your looks, not your work. All this devalues workers, it is humiliating, it can make women very depressed or angry, it causes stress and therefore absenteeism. Outline the fact that sexual harassment is about power and not about sex. Quote, in evidence, the fact that people who are seen as vulnerable in the eyes of society (divorcees, black women, junior staff) are more likely to be harassed. Point out that most harassers are men and are usually in a position of power either by virtue of their position at work, their size, their seniority, their numbers or their position in society.

Outline the law relating to sexual harassment (use Chapter 3).

Finally stress the fact that sexual harassment is a barrier to equal opportunities and that if it is not tackled it will cost the organization money in terms of absenteeism and staff replacement, not to mention the possible cost of industrial tribunal.

Links between sexual harassment and sexism[2]

Sexual harassment is a symptom of inequality at work. To raise people's awareness on women's position in society, to get people to question their assumptions and draw the link between sexual harassment and equal opportunities generally, trainers could use a questionnaire similar to the one given below for sexual harassment. Questions should relate to women's situation in society today. The answers shown here in brackets can be given out to trainees after the exercise has been done.

- What proportion of women (of working age) are in paid employment? (answer: 70 per cent)
- Are most married women in paid employment? (answer: yes)
- Do most women with school age children work? (answer: yes)

- What percentage of households have a married women working at home all day looking after two children? (answer: 5 per cent)
- How much does the average woman earn as a proportion of the average male wage? (answer: two thirds)
- How much leisure time do women have, compared with men? (answer: a third less).

The Equal Opportunities Commission (address given in Appendix 6) produces a leaflet on current statistics and a questionnaire which can be used for training.

You can also raise awareness by getting trainees to work on the following exercises (or similar ones) in small groups:

1 As you are passing through the office one day, you overhear a junior manager asking one of the secretaries if she would fetch him a cup of tea. You notice her grimace but she says nothing and gets up. It is not the first time you have observed this happening.

   Is there a problem? What is the problem? What would you do about it? How would you avoid it happening again? Would it make a difference if the two employees were on the same grade?

2 If women are non-existent in our language, they become non-existent in our minds.

   Give students a text written in sexist terms and ask them to rewrite it using gender neutral terms (replacing man-hours, manning, to a man, manmade, manhandle, chairman, continuous use of masculine pronouns e.g. 'he', 'his').

3 Role play: Have two women the butt of sexist remarks and two men making them with the group afterwards discussing what is going on. The two 'women' can be played by either men or women, as can the two 'men'.

   Example of remarks: 'I am glad you joined the team instead of Miss X, you are much nicer to look at' or 'you will enjoy our weekend meetings, they are good' (a nod and a wink) etc.

4 The following are the minutes of a staff meeting.

   Present: Mr John Smith (senior manager), Mr Paul Jones (manager, technical services), Sarah (manager, cleaning and catering), David (staff liaison/trade union representative), Di (from the finance section).

Mr Smith outlines the purpose of the meeting: to decide on cuts as the overall budget needs to be reduced.

Di outlines how the budget is allocated at present. She points out that most goes to technical services and. . .

Mr Jones interrupts to add that this was because of the huge responsibilities and tasks in his section. He deals with large numbers of men and needs to act as an emergency service if things break down. Also he has young chaps who have a bright future within the organization.

Di adds that she was going to say that a large chunk of the budget was also spent on cleaning and catering and staff welfare.

Mr Jones continues: in addition technical services need to keep pace with new technological developments.

David points out that upkeep of the bar and the new snooker room were high but that these facilities had been hard-fought for and were essential for staff morale. He added that some facilities like the dart boards needed replacing this year. On top of this women were making demands – he realized how unrealistic these were – for a holiday playscheme, which would mean using the snooker room during school holidays. The men would never agree to that.

Sarah points out that the staff in her section (mainly women) were also essential to the organization. The work the cleaners do may be invisible but you would notice it if it were not done. The catering was also central to the work of the organisation.

Mr Smith repeated Sarah's statement, starting off by saying 'Sarah's point is that . . .'

David says that there is a difference between the staff who work full time whose jobs must be protected and the catering and cleaning staff who are after all only part time workers. Also full time workers' posts are skilled.

Sarah continues: we have already cut back cleaning and catering to the bone and it's very important for the staff that . . .

David excuses himself saying he has an important phone call to make.

Di starts outlining possible ways to cut the budget.

Identify some of the sexist attitudes and remarks at this meeting. Explain why they are sexist. How would you react if you were at the meeting if you were John, if you were Paul or David, if you were Sarah or Di?

Sample exercises on sexual harassment

The questions given at the end of each exercise are simply examples of the sort of questions which could be asked of any exercise on sexual harassment.

1 Ann, a secretary, went to see her manager to complain about a member of staff.

Ann explains that he has repeatedly criticized her work, scouring it for minor defects in front of her colleagues. He used to criticize her even more when she was alone with him in his office so she now refuses to go in there and instead asks him to come into the open-plan office.

Since then he has increased her workload and asked her to work to tighter schedules. On one occasion he tore her work up, saying that the typing was not good enough. When she talked about this incident to her colleagues, he called her into his office and said she was 'gossiping'. After this she began to feel ill at work and had to take repeated sick leave. He told everyone she was unreliable. When she complained to him, he said she was difficult.

The manager asked Ann if she would like to transfer to another office in another department. She declined saying she liked her work and wanted to stay in the same office. He asked her if she would like to take this further, warning her that such action might make life difficult for her and that if she made a formal complaint, she might have to give evidence in front of others.

- Is there a problem? What is the problem?
- What do you think the manager should have done?

- How could one ensure that such incidents did not happen again? If Ann came to you how would you deal with the matter?
- Would your attitude be different if she were a man?

2 In one of the offices for which you are responsible the men have put up pictures of women dressed in nothing but suspender belts and stockings.

Since then the work of the staff in that office has deteriorated and they have taken more sick leave. There is also an increase in staff turnover. Some of the women have complained to the men in the office, but the men say the women are spoiling their fun.

- Is there a problem? What is the problem?
- Given that no one has complained to you directly, how would you deal with the situation?
- How would you prevent such a situation from arising again?

3 You are a close personal friend of your immediate boss Mr X. You know that he is going through problems in his marriage and that he is having a rough time at the moment.

One day, a woman in your office complains to you that Mr X is always asking her about her sex life, telling her she's got a good figure and on one occasion touching her breasts. She says that she is too embarrassed to make a formal complaint but wonders if you could have a private word with him.

- What is the problem?
- What do you do about it?
- What would be the consequences of you taking no action?
- How could you stop this sort of incident occurring again?

4 Below is the recording of a meeting between a member of staff and her manager.

Manager: Can you tell me what happened?
Leilah: P.J. has been constantly embarrassing me by making remarks about my dress and appearance.

Manager: What were you wearing?

Leilah: A short skirt and jumper.

Manager: Have there been any previous incidents?

Leilah: Yes.

Manager: Do you think you might have been leading him on?

Leilah: No.

Manager: Did anyone else see the incidents?

Leilah: No.

Manager: Don't you think that he might have been joking?

Leilah: I don't think so.

Manager: Well, P.J. has been working here for 25 years and no one has ever complained before. I know him well – he is a married man. I can't believe he would sexually harass anyone. Are you sure?

Leilah: Well, yes.

Manager: Do you really want me to take this further? It is a complicated procedure you know and will cost the company money. Do you really want to go through all this?

- Do you think the manager's approach was correct?
- What do you think he should NOT have asked? Explain why.
- What do you think he should have asked?

5 One of your employees comes to you to say that she will be handing in her resignation.

When you ask her for more details, she reveals that several of your male employees have the habit of referring to women as 'girls' and calling them 'love' and telling sexual jokes in their presence. She also points out that she is labelled as 'frigid' and as 'lacking a sense of humour' for not finding the jokes amusing, something which she finds very distressing. She has decided that she can no longer endure the atmosphere and has thus decided to leave.

- What is the problem here?
- What should you do about it?
- How could you prevent such a situation occurring again?

6 Your office contains employees of both sexes in roughly

equal numbers. One of your male colleagues is due to leave soon and has worked in the office for a number of years. A group of his friends start collecting money for a leaving present which will be presented to him during office hours just before he goes.

On the day of his departure the present is . . . a strip-o-gram which has been booked by a couple of men in your office. The next day one of your female colleagues threatens to resign if action is not taken against those who booked the strip-o-gram.

- What is the problem here?
- What do you think her line manager should do?
- What would you advise if she confided her intention to resign to you?
- How can this situation be avoided in the future?
- Would it have made any difference if only one woman was present at the strip-o-gram? And if no women were present?

7 Paula, a social science student, asked her tutor for an extension to the deadline of a crucial essay. Her tutor, who was in a hurry, suggested that they discuss it over lunch. Paula agreed. At lunch it become obvious that the tutor meant more than just discussing the deadline extension. He gazed into her eyes, sighed deeply, moved his chair closer, put his arm on the back of her chair and commented on her clothes and appearance.

- What should Paula do?
- What would you say to her if she came to you for advice?

8 At the office Christmas party, Margaret poured a glass of beer over a colleague who was pestering her. A week later the colleague takes out a grievance against her and she is dismissed.

- What do you think should happen in this case?
- How should the manager deal with the grievance?
- What should Margaret do after the incident?
- What should she do upon being dismissed?

9 You overhear a colleague commenting on the appearance of

151

a female colleague making sexual remarks to her and she seems distressed.

- Should you interfere?
- What action could you take?
- What would be the consequences of taking no action?

Examples of legal cases

If trainers wish to use legal cases, examples can be found using Chapter 3 or by using the Equal Opportunities Commission's case book (1989) *Towards Equality: A Casebook of Decisions on Sex Discrimination and Equal Pay 1976–1988*. Another manual which contains legal cases is *Discrimination: A Guide to the Relevant Case Law on Race and Sex* by Michael Rubenstein (1992a).

Examples of role play

Trainees can be asked to act out different roles (being the harasser, the person experiencing harassment, the manager investigating it, etc.). Others in the group can be asked to comment on the performance of those involved in the role play.

The following comments are examples that reflect some of the attitudes people could take on:

- 'I don't know what all the fuss is about. Men make passes at me, I can handle it.'
- 'I think it's very flattering.'
- 'Some people want to take all the fun out of life.'
- 'I have seen women harass men as much.'
- 'Women are asking for it.'
- 'I wish I was harassed.'
- 'Women enjoy it.'
- 'At her age she should be flattered.'
- 'I put up pictures because I admire women's bodies.'
- 'Boys will be boys.'
- 'It is easy to deal with harassment, just say no.'

- 'It's only a joke.'
- 'You can't change human nature.'
- 'Just ignore it.'
- 'Knee him in the balls, that's the answer.'
- 'She is too ugly/old to be harassed.'

You could add to this list using some of the ideas mentioned in the previous exercises.

Exercises for trade unionists

Many of the exercises given above can be used, rephrasing the questions in terms of the role of the trade union representative: How do you approach the case? What questions do you need to ask her/him? What action can you take in this individual case? What action should the union take to prevent such cases recurring?

Role play is extremely useful in learning how to deal with situations.

Trade unionists as well as advisers or indeed anyone giving advice need to learn to recognize some of the symptoms of sexual harassment: stress, anxiety, repeated absenteeism. They need to learn to avoid stereotypes in interviews. They also need to learn not to victimize those who come to them for help. All this can be practised in role play.

Exercises for advisers

Again many of the cases used above can be used or rewritten for training advisers. Questions should centre on the information which needs to be solicited and the advice which should be given.

Here again role play is essential to learn to deal with requests for help. One trainee could play the part of someone seeking help. Other trainees could comment on the performance of the person acting out the adviser's role.

Sample handouts

It is useful to provide at least the following:

- a copy of the company's sexual harassment policy or a summary of the main points;
- a copy of the government's advice on sexual harassment;
- a summary of the main legal points (summary of Chapter 3);
- a sheet of names and addresses where people can go for help: union contact, EOC, law centre, citizen's advice bureau and so on.

Notes

1 The exercises are grouped to coincide wih the order they are referred to in Chapter 7. They can of course be used in any order or combination that suits the trainer.
2 The exercises and the ones in the following section are taken from Collier 1991.

APPENDIX 6
CONTACT ADDRESSES

Advisory, Conciliation and Arbitration Services (ACAS)
27 Wilton Street
London SWIX 7AZ
0171 210 3000

City Centre Project
32–35 Featherstone Street
London EC1Y 8QX
0171 608 1338

Central Office of Industrial Tribunals (COIT)
93 Ebury Bridge Road
London SW1W 8RE
0171 730 0258

Equal Opportunities Commission
Overseas House
Quay Street
Manchester M3 3HN
0161 833 9244

Industrial Relations Services (training)
18–20 Highbury Place
London N5 1PQ
0171 354 5858

The Industrial Society (Information Service)
48 Bryanston Square
London W1H 7LN
0171 262 2401

Institute of Personnel Management
IPM House
Camp Road
Wimbledon SW19 4UW
0181 946 9100

The Law Centres Federation will give information on local centres – 0171 387 8570.

The National Association of Citizen's Advice Bureaux will provide the address of local CABs – 0171 833 2181.

Rights of Women (ROW)
52–54 Featherstone Street
London EC1Y 8RT
0171 251 6577

Women Against Sexual Harassment (WASH)
312 The Chandlery
50 Westminster Bridge Road
London SE1 7QY
0171 721 7593

BIBLIOGRAPHY

Alfred Marks Bureau (1991) *Sexual Harassment in the Office: A Quantitative Report on Client Attitudes and Experience*. Richmond-upon-Thames: Adsearch.

Allen, R. (1987) *How to Prepare a Case for Industrial Tribunal: For Claims Under the Sex Discrimination and Equal Pay Acts*. Manchester: Equal Opportunities Commission.

Bargaining Report (1990) Training on harassment, June.

Braidotti, R. (1991) *Patterns of Dissonance*. Cambridge: Polity Press.

British Broadcasting Company (BBC) (1993) *Making Advances: Helpline Report*. London: Broadcasting Support Services.

British Medical Journal (1992) Unprofessional behaviour, 305: 962.

Campaign Against Pornography (1992) Computer pornography, *CAP Newsletter*, Autumn.

Collier, J. and Collier, R. (1991) Detention of British citizens as hostages in the Gulf (letter), *British Medical Journal*, 303: 1405.

Collier, R. (1991) *Tackling Sexism and Sexual Harassment: A Guide for Changing the Workplace*. London: City Centre.

Collier, R. (1993) *Mental Rape: the Effects of Sexual Harassment*. London: City Centre.

Collins, E. (1992) Commission recommendation, *Sexual Harassment: Developing Effective Policies*. Conference Papers June 29, London: Industrial Relations Services.

Confederation of Health Service Employees (COHSE) (1991) *An Abuse of Power: Sexual Harassment in the NHS*. Banstead, Surrey: COHSE.

Crichton, M. (1994) *Disclosure*. London: Century.

Davidson, M.J. and Earnshaw, S. (1991) Policies, practices and attitudes towards sexual harassment in UK organisations, *Women in Management Review and Abstracts* 6: 15–21.

de Beauvoir, S. (1949) *The Second Sex*. London: Four Square Books.

DiTomaso, N. (1989) Sexuality in the workplace: Discrimination and harassment. In J. Hearn, D. Sheppard, P. Tancred Sheriff, and G. Burrell (eds) *The Sexuality of Organisations*. London: Sage.

Employment Department (1992) *Sexual Harassment in the Workplace: A Guide for Employers*. London: Employment Department.

Employment Trends (1992) Sexual harassment in the workplace, 513: 6–15.

Equal Opportunities Commission (EOC) (1985) *Code of Practice for the Elimination of Discrimination on the Grounds of Sex and Marriage and the Promotion of Equal Opportunities in Employment*. Manchester: Equal Opportunities Commission.

Equal Opportunities Commission (EOC) (1987) *Sex Discrimination Decisions*, no. 16 'Sexual Harassment'. Manchester: Equal Opportunities Commission.

Equal Opportunities Commission (EOC) (1989) *Towards Equality: A Casebook of Decisions on Sex Discrimination and Equal Pay 1976–1988*. Manchester: Equal Opportunities Commission.

Equal Opportunities Commission (EOC) (1993) *Some Facts About Women*. Manchester: Equal Opportunites Commission.

Equal Opportunities Review (1992a) Sexual harassment is bad for business, 43: 6.

Equal Opportunities Review (1992b) Harassment policies show growing sophistication, 46: 33.

Equal Opportunities Review Case Law Digest (1993a) Sexual Harassment Code Used. 15: 3–4.

Equal Opportunities Review Case Law Digest (1993b) Employment Appeals Tribunal Notes European Code, 17: 3.

Equal Opportunities Review Case Law Digest (1993c) Man Wins Sexual Harassment Claim, 17: 2–3.

European Commission (1991) 'Code of practice on sexual harassment', reproduced in *Equal Opportunities Review*, 41: 39–42.

European Commission (1993) *How to Combat Sexual Harassment at Work: A Guide to Implementing the European Commission Code of Practice*. Luxemburg: Commission of the European Communities.

European Community, M. Rubenstein (1988) *The Dignity of Women at Work: A Report on the Problems of Sexual Harassment in the Member States of the European Community*. Brussels: European Commission.

Bibliography

European Community (1990) 'Resolution on the protection of the dignity of women and men at work', reproduced in *Equal Opportunities Review*, 32: 29.

European Community (1991) 'Recommendation on the protection of the dignity of women and men at work', reproduced in *Equal Opportunities Review*, 32: 28–29.

Evening Standard, 'Why I will no longer go to work in a skirt', p. 23, 15 October 1991.

Guardian 2, 'Who's a Pretty Boy Then?', pp. 2–3, 21 January 1994.

Gutek, B.A. (1985) *Sex and the Workplace*. San Francisco, LA: Jossey-Bass.

Hearn, J. and Parkin, W. (1987) *Sex at Work: The Power and Paradox of Organisation Sexuality*. Brighton: Wheatsheaf, New York: St. Martins.

Herbert, C. (1992) *Sexual Harassment in Schools: A Guide for Teachers*. London: David Fulton Ltd.

Her Majesty's Inspectorate of Constabulary (1993) *Equal Opportunities in the Police Service*. London: Her Majesty's Inspectorate of Constabulary.

Holland, L. (1994) Dealing with harassment at work, *Equal Opportunities Review*, 53: 32–36.

Hurst, H. (1986) Sexual harassment: Focussing responsibility. In T. Boydell and M. Peddles (eds) *Gender and Work: A Guide to Materials for Women and Men in Organisations*. London: MSC Publications.

Incomes Data Services Study (1992) Combatting Sexual Harassment at Work, 513: 1–28.

Industrial Society (1993) *No Offence? Sexual Harassment, How It Happens and How to Beat It*. London: Industrial Society.

Institute of Personnel Management (1992) *Statement on Harassment at Work*. London: Institute of Personnel Management.

Kelly, A. (1992) Why have a sexual harassment policy? *Sexual Harassment: Developing Effective Policies*. Conference Papers June 29, London: Industrial Relations Services.

Leeds Trade Union and Community Resource and Information Centre (TUCRIC) (1983) *Sexual Harassment of Women at Work: A Study from West Yorkshire*. Leeds: TUCRIC.

Local Government Management Board (1993) *Sexual Harassment in the Workplace: An Employment Guide*. Luton: Local Government Management Board.

London Buses Ltd (1991) *Report on a Sexual Harassment Survey Undertaken at Three LBL Workplaces*. London: London Buses Ltd.

MacKinnon, C. (1979) *Sexual Harassment of Working Women: A Case of Sex Discrimination*. New Haven, CT: Yale University Press.

Millett, K. (1973) *Sexual Politics*. London: Virago Press.

National Association of Local Government Officers (NALGO) (1992) *Stop Sexual Harassment in the Workplace*. London: NALGO.

Observer (1991) Clarence Thomas: Victim of lynch mob or lecher exposed? 13 October.

Orbach, S. (1991) Liberty takers, *The Guardian*, 2 November.

Pattinson, T. (1991) *Sexual Harassment: The Hidden Facts*. London: Futura.

Phillips, C.M., Stockdale, J.E. and Joeman, L.M. (1989) *The Risks in Going to Work: The Nature of People's Work, the Risks they Encounter and the Incidence of Sexual Harassment, Physical Attack and Threatening Behaviour*. London: The Suzy Lamplugh Trust.

Pringle, R. (1988) *Secretaries Talk: Sexuality, Power and Work*. London: Verso.

Read, S. (1982) *Sexual Harassment at Work*. London: Hamlyn.

Rich, A. (1980) 'Compulsory Heterosexuality and Lesbian Existence'. *Signs* 5(4): 631–60.

Rubenstein, M. (1992a) *Discrimination: A Guide to the Relevant Case Law on Race and Sex*, 5th ed. Industrial Relations Services Report. London: Eclipse.

Rubenstein, M. (1992b) *Preventing and Remedying Sexual Harassment at Work: A Resource Manual*, 2nd ed. London: Eclipse.

Sartre, J.P. (1943) *L'Etre et le Néant*. Paris: Gallimard.

Sedley, A. and Benn, M. (1982) *Sexual Harassment at Work*. London: National Council for Civil Liberties.

Stanko, E.A. (1988) Keeping women in and out of line: Sexual harassment and occupational segregation. In S. Walby (ed.) *Gender Segregation at Work*. Milton Keynes: Open University Press.

Stonewall (1993) *Less Equal than Others: A Survey of Lesbians and Gay Men at Work*. London: Stonewall.

Times Higher Education Supplement (1992) Sexual harassment survey of students at Durham University, 27 November.

Trades Union Congress (TUC) (1983; revised in 1991) *Sexual Harassment at Work: TUC Guidelines*. London: TUC.

Transport and General Workers Union (TGWU) (1987) *Combating Sexual Harassment: A TGWU Shop Steward's Handbook*. London: TGWU.

United States Merit Systems Protection Board (1988) *Sexual Harassment in the Federal Workplace: Is It a Problem? An Update*. Washington, DC: Government Printing Office.

Wagner, K.C. (1992) Addressing sexual harassment on the job: Models of intervention and prevention, *Sexual Harassment: Developing Effective Policies*. Conference Papers June 29, London: Industrial Relations Services.

Bibliography

Wilkinson, B. (1991) Sexual harassment: An organisational challenge, *Equal Opportunities Review*, 36: 9–13.

Wilkinson, B. (1992) Implementing equal opportunities, *Equal Opportunities Review*, 46: 25–30.

Wise, S. and Stanley, L. (1987) *Georgie Porgie: Sexual Harassment in Everyday Life*. London: Pandora Press.

Women Against Sexual Harassment (WASH) (1990) *Sexual Harassment in the Workplace: A Guide to Legal Action*. London: WASH.

Women Against Sexual Harassment (WASH) (1992) Devising a sexual harassment policy, *Sexual Harassment: Developing Effective Policies*. Conference Papers June 29, London: Industrial Relations Services.

Woolf, V. (1929) *A Room of One's Own*. London: The Hogarth Press.

INDEX

Index

GENDERED WORK
SEXUALITY, FAMILY AND THE LABOUR MARKET

Lisa Adkins

Gendered Work contributes to current debates on the labour market via an exploration of the significance of sexual and family relations in structuring employment. Through detailed studies of conditions of work in the British tourist industry, it shows how men and women are constituted as different kinds of 'workers' in the labour market not only when segregated in different occupations but also even when they are nominally located in the same jobs.

This differentiation is shown to be connected to two key processes: the sexualization of women workers which locates women as sexual as well as 'economic' workers, and the operation of family work relations within the sphere of employment when women work as wives rather than waged-labourers in the context of the contemporary labour market. These two processes are then drawn together to show the ways in which labour market production is gendered. This book therefore makes an important contribution to the growing feminist literature which is exposing the deep embeddedness of gender within labour market processes and practices.

Special features
- New empirical material on the terms and conditions of typical contemporary jobs for women.
- New ways of understanding the gendered structure of the labour market.
- Reviews a range of analyses (feminist and sociological) in a constructively critical way to throw light on change and continuity in employment in the consumer society.

Contents
Introduction – Sexuality and the labour market – Family production and the labour market – Sexual servicing and women's employment – The condition of women's work – Bibliography – Index.

192pp   0 335 19296 3 (Paperback)   0 335 19297 1 (Hardback)